SUCK.

WORST-CASE SCENARIOS IN MEDIA, CULTURE, ADVERTISING, AND THE INTERNET

Suck.

WORST-CASE SCENARIOS IN MEDIA, CULTURE, ADVERTISING, AND THE INTERNET

Edited by Joey Anuff and Ana Marie Cox
Illustrated by Terry Colon

WIRED BOOKS, INC.

520 Third Street, Fourth Floor

San Francisco, CA 94107

Wired Books are distributed to the trade in the United States and Canada
by Publishers Group West and in the United Kingdom and internationally by Penguin.

First Edition

Library of Congress
Catalogue-in-publication Data

Suck : worst-case scenarios in media, culture,
    advertising & the Internet / edited by Joey
    Anuff and Ana Marie Cox ; illustrated by
    Terry Colon.
        p.   cm.
    Includes index.
    ISBN 1-888869-27-5
    1. Mass media and culture – United
States.   2. Mass media and technology –
United States.   I. Anuff, Joey   II. Cox,
Ana Marie.
P94.65.U6S83   1997
302.23'0973–dc21   97-29753
                                        CIP

Art Direction: Susanna Dulkinys
Design: Terry Colon

10 9 8 7 6 5 4 3 2 1 0

Wired Books, Inc., 520 Third Street, San Francisco, CA 94107

http://www.wiredbooks.com

Special thanks to:

T. Jay Fowler, *Suck.com's* resident production guru and ass-kicker, without whose senseless dedication and loyalty bordering on the pathological we would be lost, or at least very, very late.

Heather Havrilesky, who is not so much a co-editor as source of endless inspiration. Though it's true we're not laughing with you, we're laughing at you, it's only because we know you are, too.

Carl Steadman, the lost Suckster, who can claim responsibility for everything involved in creating Suck that required verifiable skill. If it weren't for Carl, Suck would just be a word scrawled in crayon on the *Wired* restroom walls.

Thanks also to:

Andrew Anker, Ed Anuff,
Chip Bayers, Matt Beer,
Paulina Borsook, Craig Colon,
Al Columbia, Ian Connelly,
Ashley Craddock, Sonya Geis,
Bill Goggins, Paul Haeberli,
Justin Hall, Will Kreth, Darryl Lee,
Hunter Madsen, Carrie McLaren,
Brock Meeks, Dave Moodie,
Josh Quittner, Louis Rossetto,
Jack Shafer, Owen Thomas,
Uncle Bob, Brad Wieners,
Gary Wolf, and everyone who's written for Suck.

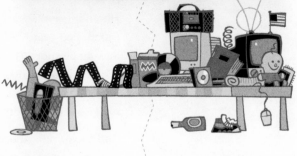

Remote Patrol

Better off Web

Politically Incoherent

Ad about You

Hyper Vexed

Pop Cult Following

Shit makes great fertilizer, but it takes a farmer to turn it into a meal. With that thought in mind, we present Suck, an experiment in provocation, mordant deconstructionism, and buzz-saw journalism. Cathode-addled netsurfers flock to shallow waters – Suck is the dirty syringe, hidden in the sand. You wanted feedback? Cover your ears and watch your back . . . it wants you too.

At Suck, we abide by the principle which dictates that somebody will always position himself or herself to systematically harvest anything of value for the sake of money, power, and/or ego-fulfillment.

We aim to be that somebody.

INTRODUCTION

Like that of a garage
band or a political platform,
the true story of Suck's genesis is probably
best left to the last best myth: something having to do with self-expression or integrity. The product of equal parts avarice and artifice, we've counted among our influences *Mad*, H. L. Mencken, *Silver Surfer*, Pauline Kael, Dorothy Parker, David Letterman, *Forced Exposure*, and The Pre-Vue Channel. We're either fantastically diverse, incredibly clued-in, or flat-out liars. As far as legends go, though, you could do worse: A couple of kids with more energy than sense, more invective than direction, nibble on the hand that feeds them, prompting it to pick up the check.

It worked. After Suck sold out, ("Does a life of concocting far-fetched ideas and seeing them through to quick completion sound appealing to you?" *http://www.suck.com/daily/95/11/21/*), and grew beyond its founders' furtive midnight side-show and into a mainstage attraction, the media came running to tell a story so attuned to the moment it should have played on Fox: The Next Big Thing, starring hipster hackers and the co-optation of rebellion, with supporting roles going to twisted loyalty and antiadvertising rants, and introducing a rising star, The World Wide Web. But grafting our underground-to-overrated trajectory into some Hudsucker fantasia is only half-right. Not only have we been unable to turn mere media attention into bona-fide talking head status, but we still haven't been able to shed the muckraking, backtalking impulses that generated the initial round of ink. You see, our history is not about escaping the mail room but going postal. If anything, the corporate largess which now keeps us in lattes has given us even more to seethe about as we toss spitballs from our gilded cage. It's an awkward posi-tion: After having told the emperor he has no clothes, we were asked to critique the wardrobe of the rest of the court.

It's been suggested that the problem was one of media, not message; amid the net's taradiddle of cultish come-ons, awkward conspiracy theories, garish kiddie porn, bomb recipes of questionable value, and transparent credit card scams, rela-tively innocuous antipropaganda like ours hardly stands a chance. Indeed, surveying the popular misconceptions about not just the net, but also about media in general, you'd be amazed what people don't know about information.

Myth: The Medium is the Message: Marshall McLuhan's infamous '60s aphorism enjoyed revitalized currency in the '90s among journalists, cultural commentators, and academics scrambling to squire "Big Picture" disquisitions on emerging digital media. Selective myopia has prevented pundits from see-ing that underneath all that media, there's still a message. But constructing a framework for understanding *Third Rock From the Sun* won't earn a book review in the *New York Review of Books* and it sure won't help fetch a MacArthur Fellowship. Worse, it's almost impossible to credibly diagnose the deteriora-tion of modern civilization – à la McLuhan – via textual analysis of *Beavis and Butt-head*. And most scholars simply lack the patience, inclination, and intelligence to think that small.

Myth: Information Wants to Be Free: This vintage cyber-punk maxim is almost as misunderstood as it is ubiquitous. Originally intended as a shorthand for the natural tendency of information, particularly useful information, to migrate from closed, proprietary loops out into open, common understand-ing, the realities of information economics eventually corrupted its authority with a lethal dose of reality. As any stockbroker would be glad to explain, information doesn't want to be free, that's just where it goes to die.

Myth: Information anxiety, a.k.a.: "There's too much information." What should have remained a disposable refrain from a Duran Duran B-side has somehow become a solemn mantra employed by career media naysayers. Much in the same way video games were once warned to be short-circuiting the neurons of button-slapping teenyboppers, a small cottage industry has developed around the one-trick concept of "information anxiety." The necessary antidote to the breathless hype-salesmen of Silicon Valley, the array of authors ever at the ready to denounce the "information revolution" seem to exist primarily to provide balance on quickly-cobbled talk show debates, their very vacuity the strongest evidence that content doesn't matter so much after all.

A quick dip into the writings of Neil Postman, George W. S. Trow, Clifford Stoll, or Theodore Kaczinski should prove satisfying to amateur anthropologists hoping to follow the anti-info meme. Witness author David Shenk, who opens his recent treatise, "Data Smog: Surviving the Information Glut," with his Kafka-esque "1st Law of Data Smog": "Information, once rare and cherished like caviar, is now plentiful and taken for granted like potatoes." Or worse, rhetoric along the lines of Dutch organizational behaviorist Geert Hofstede, as quoted in *21C*, an Australian magazine of "culture, technology and science": "The human brain can absorb only so much information. . . . If you expose people to too many changes at the same time, they are likely to get seriously ill or, in fact, die." While we recognize the potential for being extremely insulted by the new wave of information, we doubt the wound is mortal.

Myth: Information "Haves" vs. Information "Have-nots": If the internet is such a problem, why are we wiring the schools? The net is rife with Big Bad Wolves and most of them are interested in getting into Red Riding Hood's basket, not her pants. But the hustling extends off the desktop. Companies as mom-and-pop as McDonald's and Disney use give-aways and gimmicks as treats to trick valuable demographic information out the hands of those too awed by bright colors and jazzy cool stuff to notice. And their kids are targeted too. As if that weren't scary enough, on the net, little Hansel and Gretel leave a very clear trail of cookie crumbs for advertisers (or whoever) to follow all the way home. Any way you slice it, a brief study of the information economy shows a distribution curve with marketers so far ahead of everyone that arguing for net access in schools seems akin to trying to win an arms race by distributing pop guns. Furthermore, it's not as though children in all but the most destitute areas are *deprived* of information. Some studies show that 99 percent of American homes own at least one television. The internet sees the delivery of full-motion video and sound as an *enhancement,* and the ability to reliably deliver the programming you went looking for as a pleasant surprise.

Myth: Knowledge is Power: If only. Sadly, knowledge is only a lever, not a weight, and even with the longest search string around the world, will stand still until you get somebody with muscle to press "enter." This School House Rock slogan turned policy point has some value, though – it's the basis for arguments by both the information alarmists and the data democratists. Actually, we'd like to see a debate between the purveyors of information anxiety and those who carve their punditry niche out of the supposed gulf between the data-rich and informationally indigent. Then again, such a shouting match would probably be all too one-sided, if somewhat schizophrenic: information egalitarians and modern-day Medeas tend to present a united front against those who would argue that information is *neither* a virus nor a panacea, just a symptom. If either side were actually right about the power of knowledge, there'd be some value to their alliance: treating news as if it were a dangerous, even addictive, drug might be the one way to make strong, cheap, and raw information available in playgrounds across the country.

It's taken the rest of the critics a good year and half to get around to the points we were making while they were busy looking for the next Next Big Thing, and in the meantime the small battle over whether or not the web was destined to become a public access group hug or the home shopping network-meets-CNN has turned into a debate about which channel it will be on.

As for Suck's place in this formerly up-and-coming medium? Well, this book is either a testament to the web's newfound respectability, or to the fact that none of our editors has seen the sales figures from The Spot's ill-fated publishing venture. Whatever. We, the watchdogs of Way New Journalism, have jumped into the lap of the old-fashioned. We'd call it ironic, but we're not sure what that means anymore, so we'll just call it an opportunity. We figure that putting our rapacious rants between the covers of a book might finally bring down the silicon curtain that has separated the info "haves" from the info "I'd-rather-nots." We hope to detonate the media myths that mine the datasphere. And if, in the process, we manage to sow our own crop of information nescience, so be it. We're making the world safe for hypocrisy. Ours.

REMOTE PATROL

It's almost impossible
to wax indignant over the
psychically disfiguring effects
of television without being mistaken for the
lost Kaczinski brother. Meanwhile, the forces of Redmond,
Silicon Valley, and Washington are eagerly conspiring to shatter
all but the most abstract readings of television's meaning.
HDTV? A glorified computer monitor. Five hundred channels?
That's just the basic service.

Television's impending 3.0 upgrade to digital is a lush
spectacle waiting to unravel and, not coincidentally, is eerily

resonant with the digital dystopia we've come to know and love from our Intel boxes. When our televisions are running Microsoft operating systems, crunching networked Quake, spitting out invasively easy videoconferencing, and crashing in the middle of *Seinfeld,* we'll at least feel lucky that our déjà vu gets the digitally enhanced and remastered treatment.

To fully grasp the uniquely terrifying quality of tomorrow's TV-land, perhaps a bastardization of the Pandora's box mythology is required. In this version, the box opens even wider – so wide that rather than coughing up any novel pathologies, everyone and everything turns around and piles back in. The web is just an 80-million-homepage head start.

The first attempts to blur the line between the traditional media of television and the new media of the Internet have already come to pass, albeit under the aegis of trigger-happy corporate media mergeheads. The cable network MSNBC, whose PR hook from the moment it was launched was a dual presence on your Macintosh and your Magnavox, may not be the worst of both worlds, but as Howard Beagle writes in "Big Money, Little Clue," it's still a few protests shy of television revolutionized. In "Must-CNET TV?" St. Huck debugs the channel's flagship program, *The Site,* troubleshooting a rogue's gallery of industry pundits in the process. Screed Racer's "New York Minute" targets another seemingly hybrid network, NY1, "the channel where they read you the paper," and finds eerie parallels between it and the current spate of desktop newsfeed applications.

But forget about the future, here's the present. TV of today could easily be dismissed as overly democratic already, feeding the unhealthy fears, obsessions, fetishes, and appetites for dysfunction of the Barcalounge Nation. This generally translates into pure entertainment pleasure.

Take the infomercial, in particular those of the self-improvement/motivational genre. When Anthony Robbins gets going on his Ultimate Power sales pitch, it's hard not to read it as Nietzsche minus the clever, all-too-clever aphorisms. And it just seems right that the only barrier to modern philosophical doctrine comes in the form of US$169.95, payable in three easy VISA debits. "Speed Reading Between the Lines" by St. Huck dissects one of our favorite new programs, *Howard Berg's Mega Speed Reading.* If you'd bought Berg's course before you read these words, well, you'd already be negotiating a refund for this book at Borders.

But if infomercials appeal to the radically downsized egos within us all, the trend toward home video disaster footage, as documented in "Enema Vérité," is testimony to the id gone prime time. Is it an honest interest in the travails of the law-enforcement community that inspires show after show of *The World's Most Exciting Car Chases*, or an earnest desire to watch an out-of-control Winnebago ram into children, pets, and innocent motor vehicles? Would you ever watch surveillance footage for more than two seconds if you didn't know in advance that some serious bloodshed had been caught on tape? As author St. Huck surmises, and the rest of us have always suspected, death is the ultimate blooper.

Caught between the worlds of big-budget kludges and no-budget smudges, we'd book the first flight out of apologialand if someone would just market a more attractive vacation getaway. But we've heard that there is the same as here, only with shittier reception.

Enema Vérité

by St. Huck

FOR those who prefer remote control to the messier travails of actual engagement, Real TV's artful flux of affectless daredevil snuff, uplifting kitty resuscitations, heartland wedding japery, and spontaneously collapsing orchestras is the reality programming genre's richest simulation of the world beyond the screen; each weeknight, for a brief half hour, it is a life-sized map of the world.

Brokaw and Rather and all the other teleprompted bloviators constantly remind you of their mediating function: contextualizing events, conferring cultural significance upon them, they're interpreters of experience rather than the thing itself. *Real TV*'s host, John Daly, assumes a far more transparent role, segueing from segment to segment with a facile geniality that contains only trace amounts of opinion. With his animatronic blandsomeness – he looks like misplaced '70s media entity John Davidson with downsized hair, or maybe Wally Cleaver by way of Melrose Place – he hardly even registers. You get the sense that the set designer threw him in as part of the deal.

Released from the burdens of relevance and meaning, *Real TV* is free to concentrate on those sundry incidents of extreme action and emotion that make for the best television: a boxer's mother jumps into the ring and starts whacking the head of her son's opponent with the lethal heel of her shoe; a man is caught red-glanded by a hidden camera as he pisses into his coworker's coffee. What does it all mean? Who cares? *Real TV* even resists the moralizing that the tabloids and the talk shows indulge in to rationalize their salaciousness. An event's "realness"

alone justifies its presentation.

Of course, *Real TV*'s version of the "real" is paradoxical; the real, it implies, is anything that's spontaneous, unscripted, unmediated. This last value is the troublesome one. If *Real TV* subscribed to it completely, it would have nothing to broadcast. But the fact that life becomes less real the moment anyone – amateur or professional – starts to videotape it is something that *Real TV* is happy to work around. For its purposes, realness as a stylistic trope is enough, as the show's introductory animation demonstrates: instead of showing images of actual events, it simply cycles through myriad instantiations of the word *real* done in all the usual-suspects cybergrunge typefaces used to dress up drivel as DIY.

But the hip typography is just graphic foreplay. *Real TV*'s primary means of establishing its authenticity are more corporeal; in a good week, you're likely to witness several actual deaths: skiers crashing, surfers snapping their necks, daredevils falling off airplanes. The realness of such scenes is obvious; even if an event is carefully choreographed, with multiple cameramen positioned in advance to capture its details, a fatal outcome is almost always spontaneous: death is the **ultimate blooper.** ....

Face Death
http://www.facedeath.com/
The future of the Internet is shopping, experts predict. The Face Death online videomart offers everything the amateur necrophiliac could ask for, conveniently organized into three intuitive categories: "Death," "Death & Dying," and "Caligula." Well, "intuitive" from a student psychopath's perspective, anyway. Though that might be unfair, considering the socially responsible subtext hinted at in the blurb copy accompanying the featured titles, "The Many Faces of Death: The intent of this explicitly graphic Shockumentary is to increase your awareness of the tragic true-life horrors that can happen to the unaware. These tragedies can happen to any of us, any day. . . . Beware!!! Spread the word, help others to understand. Stop the madness!" Funny, that was our excuse.

Nonetheless, the surveillance-camera footage that *Real TV* features is even more compelling. While it generally lacks the mortal consequences of the death scenes, its spontaneity factor is greater. Indeed, surveillance cameras have given us a whole new genre of tedious suspense – call it enema vérité. If you point a camera at a cash register long enough, eventually shit happens; the suspicious-looking character enters the store, leaps the counter, and starts smashing his fist into the clerk's head when she doesn't follow his instructions fast enough.

Even when *Real TV* presents videotape as striking as that, it never dwells on it for too long. To do so would be to risk contemplation – and if viewers started thinking, they might stop watching. In this respect, *Real TV* is a lot like MTV: the news as music video, a shifting stream of imagery designed to resist meaning via constant retinal agitation. It's no mere oversight that the show never mentions when the events it presents actually occurred; that jockey could have been trampled yesterday, or a week ago, or maybe even a couple of years ago. It really doesn't matter, because *Real TV* is a timeless environment, where everything happens in the moment. The closest it ever comes to a sense of history is when it replays a particularly compelling piece of videography over and over – the past as rewind button.

Geography is slightly more apparent, but only in the most superficial ways. Most often it's invoked to add realness to a segment; videotape from foreign, less mediated countries is presented, in the tradition of *Mondo Cane*, as inherently more authentic than that which comes from the United States. In addition, it's used as a kind of narrative shorthand that eliminates the need for more satisfying explanation: Why are those cops kicking and punching their prisoners so brazenly? Oh, they're Russian cops.

Beyond these uses, *Real TV*'s producers have little interest in geography; they understand that the TV nation is a nation of one. And, thus, unlike other shows in the reality genre, *Real TV* makes no attempt to create (or even acknowledge) a sense of community. The studio audience of *America's Funniest Home Videos* is dispensed with, as is the bank of telephone volunteers of *America's Most Wanted*. In the *Real TV* universe, the most important elements are the viewer and the segments; intrusive talking-head shots of Daly and the show's reporters are kept to a minimum. The voyeur prefers self-service.

Of course, the passive Peeping Tomism that *Real TV* encourages has its downside – in time the show could run out of material. Certainly there's no shortage of people ready to videotape mishaps and catastrophes; one recent *Real TV* episode featured a segment submitted by a man who kept his camera diligently trained on an icy intersection as car after car came along, spun out, and crashed into things. Instead of trying to warn motorists of the potential danger, the man was content to

provide jovial, couch-potato commentary for his masterpiece's audio track: "Oh, no, here comes another!"

But when we all become voyeurs and videographers, who will be left to perform the stupid high jinks worth capturing on tape? On another recent episode, *Real TV* featured footage of a small plane flying underneath a suspension bridge. Accompanying this spectacle came an uncharacteristic moral proscription from Daly: *Real TV* was not showing this footage to glorify its creators, he admonished, but rather to warn people about the illegal and dangerous nature of stunts like that. But this isn't *Hard Copy*ish hypocrisy; the real message underlying the sentiment is clear: please, please, please try this at home – we need the tape!

New York Minute

by Screed Racer

*"News Feud Escalates," CNNfn
(October 10, 1996)*

*http://cnnfn.com/hotstories/companies/
9610/11/tw_murdoch_pkg/index.htm*

*"The battle began when Time Warner
Chairman Gerald Levin told News Corp.
Chairman Rupert Murdoch that MSNBC
had been selected for carriage on Time
Warner's cable system in the city, rather
than the Fox News Channel."*

In an era of breakneck media merging,
battling moguls comes as a breath of fresh
air. So what if we're robbed of the satisfaction of having a favorite to root for?
Murdoch sues Time Warner. Time Warner
sues Giuliani. All for the sake of the good
news-loving people of NYC. Right?

About NY1

http://pathfinder.com/NY1/about/intro.html
Every corporation needs its own creation
myth, and cable networks are no exception.
Just as every MTV intern learns that the
dawn of human history commenced with
the airing of the Buggles' "Video Killed the
Radio Star," we're pretty sure NY1's corporate creed reverberates through the halls
and heads of 460 West 42nd Street. "NY1
News, Time Warner's 24 hour news channel, was launched on September 8, 1992 at
1 pm. The anchor that day was Leslie Devlin
and the first thing seen on the air was the
NY1 Minute. The highlight of our first hour
was an interview with Mayor David
Dinkins." Of course it was.

IF NO news is good news, then good news is torture.

Dependence on news – and lots of it – nettles the infojunkie as
powerfully as nicotine addiction hounds the smoker. But news consumption is no more an addiction than eating, breathing, or playing Nintendo
64 – like those functions, it's required for survival. PointCast knows that,
and so does Rupert Murdoch. But does Time Warner's Gerald Levin
know it? If he did, you wouldn't be reading this right now. You'd be
watching New York 1.

Debuting on Time Warner cable in 1992, New York 1 began with
the dream of cheaply produced local news and grew into something even
better: locally produced cheap thrills. Very cheap. But what New York 1
lacks in cash it makes up for in heart. Its reporters lug their own cameras
through Gotham's tough streets. And the channel's musical themes,
pounded out on the pluckiest of synthesizers, are surely the work of an
artist driven by the promise of bus fare home. This damn-the-aesthetics-
full-news-ahead attitude ("Fuck it, we've got a town to inform. I'm wearing my ball cap and Jams!") pervades the operation – right down to the
unkempt writer-drones always seen toiling in the background behind the
anchor. Their day involves scanning wire dispatches, typing stories, and
roaming aimlessly for the camera.

Such devotion from writers, reporters, and MIDI devices could
only be inspired by a charismatic leader – stern in his demands, stoic
with praise, inspirational in his work ethic. For New York 1, this guiding

figure is the Sony LMS 1000. After taping multiple story segments and filing them in the Sony, the channel creates each newscast on the fly with a mix of as many live and canned reports as events or energy levels warrant. Giuliani not pissy today? Run the last half hour again. Blood hits pavement somewhere? Cut in a live feed, then back to the Weekday Transit Outlook. Toot, toot! The "fresh *because* it's frozen" slogan isn't just for bagels anymore.

Watch New York 1 for just one hour – if you have that much restraint – and you'll recognize what Levin has not. Local content base, push platform, automation, numbing repetition . . . doesn't feel familiar yet? Try holding a mouse in your hand.

Unlike MSNBC, which only uses the web, NY1 is the web's future, making the recent launch of NY1's website both recursive and redundant. Sure, the actual web isn't up to the achievements of this web-in-coaxial-clothing, but we've actually tried to clickthrough on the 1-800-Rest-In-Peace ads. (Is there any doubt as to the utility of such a service, which promises "tasteful bouquets for sensitive occasions"?)

The gaping content maw that greets most new media ventures has been handily conquered by the wily NY1 staff. Tune in forty-one minutes past the hour between seven and ten o'clock and you'll see an anchor

point out whatever stories she found interesting that day in the newspapers. Morning anchor **Roma Torre** flags articles she likes with Post-It notes and then ad-libs, occasionally about her kids. One summer morning Torre mispronounced "Gennadi Zyuganov," then apologized, "Sorry, I don't follow Russian politics." She's also spoken with pride of "Uncle Joe Torre. Get it? Torre . . . Roma Torre? Ha-ha. No, no relation, just kidding. Anyhow, in the *Daily News* today. . . ."

"In the Papers" is a hypnotic piece of performance art. Mention New York 1 to people on the street, and those who've heard of it will say, "Isn't that the channel where they read you the paper?" In new media, you call that a budding brand image.

Even the most cagey CEO – let alone one whose books contain more debt than a Kemp wet dream – could overlook this potential new media treasure. Levin must not know that PointCast is the model to beat right now. And what is New York 1 but a screensaver for your television?

Roma Torre
http://pathfinder.com/NY1/about/bios/torre
.html
"Roma Torre was born just in time to see her mother hauled off to jail. It was a celebrated case involving freedom of the press. Marie Torre, Roma's mom, became the first reporter in the country to go to jail protecting a source of information. It was a ten day sentence." We plead the Fifth.

Big Money, Little Clue

by Howard Beagle

FIGURING that all we know about journalism we learned from the *Mary Tyler Moore Show*, late-movie showings of *His Girl Friday* and our officemate's repeated references to *Network*, it's tough to cite the source for the only rule we really try to follow: in times of national and/or personal tragedy, raillery must wait twenty-four hours. We probably made it up ourselves.

Still, in face of Flight 800, we restrained the temptation to crack a joke. MSNBC, on the other hand, actually came off as one.

To say the joint venture between Microsoft and NBC "took off" would be tasteless, and cruel to those unfortunate enough to have taken a seat in front of the televised disaster. At least we can be reassured, in our own flight from the wreckage, that few would accuse us of shooting down something that was already so obviously dead in the water.

The dual calamities couldn't have been better timed if Faye Dunaway had scheduled them. Both the airline and the cable industries rely on decades-old vehicles, and both are badly in need of public scrutiny. But do we really have to watch?

Despite the scale of loss, the Flight 800 story didn't actually amount to much news – there's still very little new to report, after all. And, far from defining it as a contender, MSNBC's on-the-minute coverage of the event seemed opportunistic and amateur – a desperate attempt to steal some of CNN's Challenger-wrought mettle. When the fledging service was announced, we expected a scrappy cross between ESPN-2 and The Learning Channel, with a healthy dose of Redmond propaganda sweetening the mix. So on that Wednesday night, we could only wonder why MSNBC was covering plane crashes, not Netscape crashes.

The Ziff-Davis-produced *The Site* ("the revolution will be televised") chose, too, to profit in other people's misery – both the plane crash victims' and ours. Thursday's program included a Yahoo! rep demonstrating how to find digitized photos of the disaster (which he alternatively described as "awful," "horrible," and "sickening," but then kept showing us more), and a staffer giving a report of what he found on alt.disaster.aviation after the crash. Devoid of interpretation or analysis, *The Site* only served to heighten the spectacular nature of the tragedy – talking heads describing what they saw on their computer screens, which largely consisted of firsthand accounts of people watching CNN.

To those still awake after *The Site*'s Monday debut, this lack of contextualization should come as no surprise. The show focused on another crash: the recent poor performance of tech stocks. *The Site*'s report didn't speculate on why the market was going down (the commentator seemed quite smug to simply report that it was, in fact, going down). Then again, the program segment in and of itself is a pretty clear indication of why the market's heading south.

We thought that it was the no-hands mouse that provided an "integrated media experience," but Bill Gates has promised that MSNBC will. Some may be wary when those producing programs about the future are the same tech-media conglomerates that are bent on selling us their future products, but we look forward to the day when Microsoft's new network merges with Microsoft's last one, so that MSN/GENIe is a desktop icon in Windows NT. And what's to stop Ziff-Davis from making *The*

NBC and Microsoft Announce Joint Venture

http://www.nbc.com/announce/press.html

"Advances in digital technology will give people new control over news and information. They will be able to call up news on demand, at their convenience. They will be able to customize their news service. They will be able to watch breaking news on TV and then be able to get more in-depth information on things of interest to them online," says Bill Gates in the MSNBC launch press release.

Unfortunately there's nothing digital about cable TV. How far will US$220 mil get your fledgling cable network vision in the last years of the twentieth century? Pretty far, if you spend it wisely. MSNBC has been applying a technique pioneered by Rupert Murdoch, paying cable providers to carry the channel, often bumping networks like C-SPAN and the Sci-Fi Channel in the process. Maybe when all is said and done, money is the ultimate science fiction, anyway.

Site not two sites but one, seamlessly blending its TV programming and webvertisement for same? Once we've achieved digital convergence, the content may be the same old shit, but at least we'll have one less crap channel to click past.

It's no longer a matter of whether or not the revolution will be televised – though there's some question as to its ability to make it past a V-chip. What remains most salient is that the television will not be revolutionized.

Speed Reading Between the Lines

by St. Huck

The Infomercial Index

*http://www.magickeys.com/infomercials/
index.html*

The smell of a new car. High-pressure sales tactics. Quick, painless money loss. Think these pleasures are only available at your local Buick dealer? Think again. From the Lark Scooter to Secret Hair, the Infomercial Index guarantees that you'll never again fail to take advantage of an opportunity to misuse your credit card, providing convenient pricing and ordering information for a diverse selection of preposterous horseshit. "Find the information for that infomercial you scribbled down and now can't find by using . . . The Infomercial Index."

THE true bandwidth bottleneck of the Information Age is the sluggardly rate of human comprehension. And while the telecommunications industry is doing absolutely nothing to solve this problem, Howard Stephen Berg, the latest star of Kevin Trudeau's Vantage Point infomercial series, has stepped up to offer his Mega Speed Reading Program as the path to transcend the limits of our bundled wetware.

Dubbed the World's Fastest Reader by that ultimate arbiter of esoteric supremacy, the *Guinness Book of World Records*, the pudgy prelector assimilates entire books in about the same amount of time it takes the average page-turner to get through a typical Nicholson Baker footnote. But to describe what Berg does merely as "speed reading" or even "mega speed reading" fails to do justice to his audacious, absolutely straight-faced performance. With his mesmerizing, back-and-forth hand motions and superefficient page-turning technique, Berg appears as nothing less than an ArtiScan incarnate.

The surprisingly charismatic Berg resembles a blend of *Seinfeld*'s Newman and the turtlelike Truman Capote, but his corpulent appearance belies his supreme salesmanship skills. As he scans the multigigabyte hard drive of his brain, he is in the habit of tilting his melon-sized head backward and rolling his eyes upward as if to consult the crib notes he's pasted to the ceiling; in moments like that, he somehow manages to project both a vivid sense of mastery and a phenomenal if-that-guy-can-do-it-so-can-I quotient. In addition, Berg possesses a world-class infomercial voice: an insistent but affable nasal whine, resonant with the goatish diphthongs and sharp contractions of Brooklyn street corners. He's abrasive enough to break through the Teshian white noise of fifty channels, and once he's snared the restless channel-surfer's attention, his fast-paced, giggle-prone patter proves remarkably compelling.

The infomercial itself is a stripped-down, old-school huckster's affair. There's no unbelievably enthusiastic audience, no dubious, talking-head testimonials, no hokey Premiere transition tricks – just two impeccably groomed men behind an anchorman's desk, discussing the many benefits of reading really, really, really fast. In the first several minutes, a winning formula is established: Trudeau gestures emphatically, gives Berg a book to read, watches pop-eyed as Berg passes his hand over the book's pages, then quizzes Berg about what he just read. After this initial sequence, they repeat the process four more times with different books; soon, the requisite thirty minutes have been filled.

While Trudeau's inexhaustible reservoir of incredulousness – "I can't believe he's reading!" – begins to controvert his self-proclaimed status as the world's leading memory expert, one has to admire the dogged simplicity of the show's approach. One trick, repeated over and over and over, until it achieves a kind of irrational credibility. In the best infomercial tradition, Berg never attempts to explain his technique; he simply says that his program unlocks one's "natural ability" to read quickly. For the lazy, he offers the assurance that his program takes less than four hours to learn. For the tenuously literate, he explains that even the severely brain damaged and the blind have benefited from his instruction!

If such claims begin to sound a little, uh, unprecedented, one has to remember: Berg is a revolutionary, a linguistic maverick constantly demonstrating his break from traditional notions of literacy. There's his penchant for introducing wonderfully euphonious coinages such as *reciprocant.* Or his tendency to shun conventional pronunciation in lieu of more evocative variants – *vignette* with a hard *g* appears to be a favorite. Most of all, of course, there's his ability to digest whole chapters in seconds, and then recall their entire contents with remarkable accuracy.

Well, maybe remarkable is too strong a word. In fact, in the one instance where I was able to check the accuracy of Berg's comprehension, I was fairly disappointed. It occurs when Trudeau hands him a copy of Dale Carnegie's *How To Win Friends and Influence People;* coincidentally, I happened to have that title in my own vast library of self-help literature. Responding to Trudeau's request to summarize the book's sixth chapter, which he has just spent several seconds reading, Berg explains that Carnegie tries to cheer up a depressed postal employee he knows by telling him how important he is. However, when I checked the book's text, I found that Carnegie actually characterizes the postal worker as a "stranger," not someone he knows, and as "bored" rather than "depressed." Most significantly, instead of telling the man how important he is, Carnegie simply says, "I certainly wish I had your head of hair."

Given the gimcrack élan of Berg's entire presentation, however, a tiny comprehension mishap like that hardly even registers. After all, isn't Berg essentially the Evel Knievel of speed reading, performing high-risk stunts no other bookworm has even dared to attempt? As such, he's bound to crash now and then. And since his Mega Speed Reading program takes less than four hours to complete, what do you have to lose except a few missed episodes of *Cops* and *Real TV*?

Well, US$169.95 if you actually pay for it; luckily, I obtained a review copy.

Following the course's instructions, I picked a book to practice with – *Yes, I Can: The Story of Sammy Davis, Jr.* – then determined my current reading speed, which turned out to be a relatively torpid 375 words per minute. Not that I was too dismayed about this embarrassing failure of intellectual prowess. Soon, I knew, I would be turning pages as fast as a callus-fingered Evelyn Wood veteran.

As it turns out, that much is true. I have totally mastered Berg's page-turning technique; in fact, if I forsake the reading part, I can actu-

ally flip something like 110 pages a minute. In addition, I also found Berg's advice about using one's hand to pace one's eye helpful. The rest of his techniques, however, either eluded me or were so obvious or general that they hardly qualified as "revolutionary breakthroughs." Here's a representative sampling from his bag of tricks: read backwards, read passages you're already familiar with at a high speed, always study a book's table of contents and index, use mnemonics to remember things.

Reading backwards appears to be Berg's unique selling proposition; to his credit, he manages to present the idea with a fairly convincing measure of sincerity, even when rationalizing the feasibility of such an endeavor by explaining that many languages, including Hebrew and some Asiatic ones, are read backwards. Of course, this isn't true at all – such languages are simply read right to left, which to their readers *is* forward. But maybe it's the adherence to such common sense that keeps me a slow-witted mouth reader while Berg is making TV shows, moving product, and captivating the likes of Regis and Kathie Lee. In short, if you have no need to approach reading as a sequential activity, reading backwards apparently works just fine.

Unfortunately, I showed no aptitude for that skill, which is perhaps why at the end of the program my reading speed increased only marginally, to five hundred words per minute. (A full hundred words less than the brain-damaged woman who took Berg's course, I'm somewhat embarrassed to admit.) Maybe I simply wasn't concentrating hard enough. Certainly, the course's US$169.95 price tag was a constant distraction. How many people, I kept wondering, had paid that price only to hear superficial comprehension tips or Berg enthusiastically shouting the index of some unnamed psychology book: "Dog! Drooling! Pavlov! Russian! Psychologist! Salivating!"

Actually, that surreal moment was probably worth US$5 itself, putting the total value of the package at around US$20. If cost of goods precludes such a low price, maybe Berg can strike a deal with a publishing house, or even a coalition of them, to subsidize Mega Speed Reading's production and marketing so it's affordable to everyone. Imagine an entire nation of speed readers, devouring the likes of *Infinite Jest* in a single bus ride. A tiny percentage of the profits from a revitalized publishing industry could turn Berg into the next Bill Gates.

Of course, such a prospect is based on the notion that Mega Speed Reading actually works; I guess the infomercial strategy is a safer way to play it. But why stop there? If Berg's program offers mostly entertainment value, why not turn it into programming? Fledgling networks like WB and UPN are starved for innovative content: Berg, Trudeau, and a few other infomercial superheros like Don Lapre and Marshall Sylver could be the A-Team (or B-Team, adjusting for depreciation) of the '90s! Instead of using guns and muscle to rescue hapless has-beens like Danny Bonaduce, they could simply teach their rotating guest stars how to get out of tricky jams and foil diabolical adversaries by reading really fast, employing lethal memory tricks, placing tiny classified ads, and practicing self-hypnosis.

Must-CNET TV?

by St. Huck

THE other night, as I endured the blandly manic, open-mike-caliber punditry of videogame reject **Dev,** the secret purpose of *The Site* suddenly occurred to me: to make the web appear as insipid and irrelevant as possible, in the hope that this might spur magazine sales. Given that publications like *The New Yorker*, *The Wall Street Journal*, *The Sporting News*, and a dozen or so others are *The Site*'s most frequent advertisers, I probably should have divined this sooner; perhaps I was simply overcome by the show's infectious mood of antianalytic somnabulance.

Of course, *The Site* is actually pretty good at producing the kind of hobby-oriented, up-with-people stories that CompuServe's member magazine pioneered in the early '90s. Did you know, for example, that amateur genealogists use the web? And technologically spry seniors? And forgetful folks who've lost track of their uncles and ex-boyfriends? Well, it's true!

Only in that strange state of digital delusion known as Jon Katz's 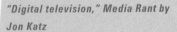 could such stuff pass as an "important breakthrough in broadcast journalism." While that realm's addled emperor calls *The Site* the net's "own evening news," people who pay more than cursory attention to the show are more apt to liken it to an endlessly repeated Buzz Bin video: segments that seem overly familiar the first time around become so much televisual surf upon the sixth Siting. In this respect, the show does achieve a new-media breakthrough of sorts: it proves that it's now possible, in this age of pervasive syndication and heavy rotation, to recy-

cle the "news" without anyone noticing – or at least caring that much. Sure, *The Site*'s producers could cut down on the repeats by reducing the show's running time to half an hour, or airing it less frequently, but then, as Site reporter Craig Miller explains, they'd only be able to run ten commercials per episode instead of twenty.

With a pick-up-your-phone-and-call-now pitch punctuating every segment, it's only fitting that *The Site*'s set resembles an infomercial's version of a newsroom more than it does an actual one: busy infobees buzzing at their workstations, self-consciously visible camera crew members, a jazzy anchor desk, and plenty of neon in the background. Soledad O'Brien, the show's quintessential Lisa-unit host, appears right at home in this milieu; as she wanders toward the set's coffee bar to banter with Dev, you almost expect her to break into an impromptu demonstration of some new high-tech kitchen gadget.

Instead, she simply deploys an impressive arsenal of facial expressions and gestures: the judicious-moment-of-analysis lip purse, the quizzical head tilt, the uh-huh-uh-huh-I'm-not-buying-it smile. She has the kind of slightly above-average intelligence that works so well on TV, and the smooth self-possession the job requires – but not for a moment do you believe that such a savvy careerist has any real interest in a time waster like the web. You can see in her eyes the unspoken question (that we ourselves have grown tired of asking), Why?

Compared with the polished O'Brien – or even Monday Night Football's Dan Dierdorf – *The Site*'s Denise Caruso often comes across as a bit brusque, but at least her interest in her subject is apparent. Watching her interview William Gibson about his new novel *Idoru*, for example, you get the feeling she's actually read the thing – and probably some other books too.

The rest of *The Site*'s supporting cast add little to the mix. Nervous young spokesmodels from Yahoo! demonstrate on a nightly basis how hard it can be to actually say something meaningful about a site instead of simply labeling it "cool." The computer-generated Dev is exactly as annoying as you'd expect a real guy named Dev to be. And about the most you can say for Jim Louderback is that for someone who's primarily a print journalist, he sure is well-groomed. To be fair, Louderback does get the show's toughest assignment: showing off new software. Not surprisingly, his tedious reports make it exceedingly clear why developers at Comdex staff their booths with jugglers, comedians, and off-duty strippers; demonstrating software is one of the most boring pastimes in the world. Eventually, one imagines, the software reviewer will evolve into the computer show's version of the zany weatherman: a cartoonish dolt who leavens the information he delivers with at least an equal dose of "comic relief." Louderback, a kind of preppy version of Kato Kaelin, simply lacks the presence for this difficult task.

As for Cliff Stoll, well . . . Stoll is so objectionable he gets his own paragraph. Until recently, I'd always thought it was pretty near impossible to give the long-petrified Andy Rooney less than his due, but I believe Ned Brainard recently accomplished that miraculous feat by comparing Stoll to the still alarmingly lifelike curmudgeon. For all his rote sourpussery, Rooney at least occasionally manufactures a point now and then; the squirmy Stoll is so scattered he barely manages a smudge.

Taking unpreparedness as a seeming badge of honor, he invariably scrunch-faces and tiny-sighs and shoulder-shrugs his way toward some incomprehensible mishmash of his one best-selling notion: machines are OK, sort of, but the real world – with all its, um, people, and, uh, stuff – is where it's at. Like some Dr. Seuss character who never quite made it out of beta, the wistful stargazer is filled with an inexhaustible reservoir of love for humanity – at least through the mediating mechanisms of print and TV. But I know some folks who live in his neighborhood, and they say in the flesh he's actually a bit standoffish.

At the moment, *The Site*'s own true identity is similarly ambiguous. Yes, this is the age of Cuisinart culture, and sometimes an unprecedented blend – the PBS-style cooking show crossed with *American Gladiators*, say – results in an **inspired addition** to the canon. But haven't we **already learned** what you get if you mix *The Evening News* with the *Today Show* with the *McLaughlin Group* with *Siskel and Ebert*, and you limit the subject to the online world, and you skimp on the point of view and the budget?

Frankly, I've yet to hear any actual TV viewer say, "I want something like CNET, only lots more of it." Unfortunately, that seems to be all we're going to get.

Iron Men

http://www.ikonic.com/who/ganderson/ironchef.html

As this fan page notes, "It's American Gladiators-meets-Julia Child. The MC stands at the center of the 'Kitchen Stadium,' as jump cuts across the day's weapons begin: peppers, onions, foie gras." If someone at MSNBC had devised a method of shoehorning an Internet angle into Iron Chef, would our indigestion be any less profound?

CNET

http://www.cnet.com/

If books about the Internet can sell by the truckload, and television about books charts a few starters each season, why not television about computers? CNET, the original cybervariety TV show, deserves credit for, at the very least, spreading the message to a couch-locked audience that a bit is a very small thing, indeed. CNET's raison d'être is sound enough: when the masses finally trade in their televisions for workstations, the only guarantee is that they'll need tech support and lots of it, even if they don't.

BETTER OFF WEB

Everybody seems
to agree: 99 percent
of the web is bit vomit, and
the other 1 percent simply isn't worth the
stomach-pounding gag reflex. The average website's design is
an affront to the eye on par with the medieval use of the white-
hot poker. Civilizations rise and fall, lavish cultures emerge, and
new languages take form, all in the time it takes for most web
pages to download. Intelligent, reasoned discourse is rarer
than Bill Gates sightings at Seattle soup kitchens. It's a soap-

box for swellheads, airheads, and shitheads. It's the square root of the lowest-common-denominator. And so on.

Obviously, everything is going exactly as planned. It's not just the impeccable product pitch, redolent with palpable excitement and an honest-to-goodness danger rarely associated with retail products, much less consumer electronics. The web, as it exists right now, is a problem – and a "nontrivial" one at that, as a software engineer might put it. Which just happens to make it the ultimate platform in a world where people no longer buy, sell, and trade products, but "solutions" (cf. "Solutions for a small planet" – IBM ad, circa 1997.)

The negative press, be it dismissive, disillusioned, or disingenuous, is as much an aspect of the ubiquitous solution-salesmanship as any IBM Business Suite or Netscape Commerce Server – some people just prefer coding in English over Java. It's crucial that the web, as a medium, lose its cool – and every commentator that oh-so-thoughtfully observes that the web won't feed the poor, your cat, or your head is only easing this transition along. After all, HBO couldn't care less whether you think TV in general is the shit; they're just hoping you watch Dennis Miller. (cf. "It's not TV, it's HBO.") If one conglomerate owned the web it might be different, but until Microsoft cuts that check, everybody will instead be claiming to sell that rarest of items, the much-discussed and seldom-seen one percent. And the consensus on the other 99 percent will remain unchallenged.

CHARACTER ASSASSINATION
page 26

Observing that even the most precocious child won't lose all his teeth in a single day, the Duke of URL's "Character Assassination" reflects on the wrenching impact of Bob Dole's attempt to co-opt the web as a youth outreach tool. Beyond observations on the web's steady decline toward the prosaic, though, the more provocative phenomenon of mainstream media simultaneously denigrating and appropriating geek culture is noted and cautiously feted.

The egregious commercial corruption of the search engine market and the Machiavellian power plays of industry giants AOL, Netscape, and Microsoft are canvassed in "Search and Destroy" and "Murky Brown," respectively. Both essays are grounded in the observation that traffic is the hard currency of the web, and the ability to attract and divert it is the most meaningful power available to any online contender. "Search and Destroy" reflects on one notable instance of a search engine outfit, Open Text, attempting to abuse this power by rigging its listings for dollars, and the ensuing outrage. "Murky Brown," meanwhile, concerns itself with the battle amongst digital titans to own the all-important first click, with an implicit message best expressed by a Swahili proverb: "When elephants

SEARCH AND DESTROY
page 29

MURKY BROWN
page 32

fight, it is the grass that suffers."

One of Suck's favorite full-contact sports – the site review – is represented in Ann O'Tate's "Wiping the Slate Clean," an early exercise in troubleshooting Michael Kinsley's Microsoft-funded Slate, which also meditates on the knee-jerk animus aimed at Slate's putatively insolent trespass. Moving from old-school journalism to old-school institutions, we turn our attention to less virtual strains of information science with Dilettante's "Ex Libris," a persuasive case for the conservation of that archaic repository for anachronistic media – the library.

It's possible that the web really is as fiercely dehumanizing as its critics claim. Perhaps the mark of the beast, rather than being a UPC code embedded on our foreheads, will instead manifest as an IP address, or at least a mandatory URL on everyone's business card. If so, our metaphysical bobbing for apples, our biting into the fruit of networked knowledge, might be better served by a sober reflection on our primal hungers. We may find that our frenzied cravings for a single-bite theory for truth, wisdom, and a robust stock portfolio is doomed. Doomed, that is, without a healthy and voracious appetite for worms.

WIPING THE SLATE CLEAN
page 35

EX LIBRIS
page 38

Character Assassination

by Duke of URL

TWA Flight 800 Disaster Cover-Up

http://www.all-natural.com/twa800.html

Suppressed. Hidden. Denied. Covered up.
Stringing these words together for a query
on the average search engine would likely
yield too many results to handle. On the
web, bad information only dies when by
some strange turn of events it becomes
official. Thus, we expect a long life span
for the TWA Flight 800 Disaster Cover-Up
archive, laden as it is with the uproarious
name-dropping of Pierre Salinger and point-
ers to grainy photos. If it wasn't out there,
it wouldn't be in here.

*"The CIA and Crack: Evidence Is
Lacking of Alleged Plot,"* **The
Washington Post** *(October 4, 1996)*

http://www.washingtonpost.com/wp-srv/
national/daily/oct/4/ciacontra.htm
For unbelievers, the easy availability of the
San Jose Mercury News' "Dark Alliance"
feature on the web *(http://www.mercury
center.com/drugs/)* just proves their point.
But it's not just annotated potboilers that
find their home online – rebuttals like that
of *The Washington Post* get equal airtime, if
not equal traffic. The *Post* argues that what
was new in Gary Webb's article was wrong,
and what was right wasn't new. Though the
claims that crack-dealing protagonist
"Freeway Ricky Ross" couldn't have been
single-handedly responsible for the crack
epidemic, with or without CIA aid, may ring
true to longtime pipe-smokers, the *Post*
reporters' footloose zeal in exonerating the
intelligence community predictably struck
some web theorists as evidence of a "dark
alliance" in its own right.

AS the twenty-four hour global syndication of *Mad About You*
completes its course, one may doubt that television ever put a
bad idea to rest. But once the echo is tuned out, a subtle system of television punctuation becomes discernible, replete with ellipses and question marks performing much of the grunt work of stringing us along, one
segment at a time.

A rare instance of a solid-period, end-of-story, full-stop moment
took place in the first presidential debate when Bob Dole croaked his
URL to a bemused electorate. If the web had ever been cool, if it could
have even laid claim to the illusion of cool, it died that moment. At some
moment between Dole's muttering of *www* and his failure to include the
dot between *dolekemp* and *org*, the web became conclusively, incontro-
vertibly lame.

Being associated with a loser can hobble those of mightiest
stature, a social curse seen time and again; witness the plight of the
unfortunates linked to Mark Fuhrman, Louis Farrakhan, Joe Esterhaz,
and Newt Gingrich. And when misery rains, it pours. Even before Dole's
flub, TV programming has shown a seismic shift in attitude toward the
digital grotto.

New Yorker legal observer Jeffrey Toobin – in the context of his
coverage of the O. J. trial, no less – dismissed the web on Tom Snyder's
show as a hotbed of addled Flight 800 theories. *Wired, New Yorker*,
and *Economist* digital pundit John Heilemann found himself the fall guy
for the web on a Charlie Rose discussion of "hysterical, irresponsible"
CIA-crack connection rumors. Even blow-up-doll-made-flesh Cindy

"The State Folk Dance Conspiracy: Fabricating a National Folk Dance," **Old Time Herald** *(Spring 1995)*
http://www.access.digex.net/~jmangin/ sqdconsp.html
"Modern Western square dance clubs are coordinating across the U.S. to have square dancing declared the state folk dance of all fifty states. At the time of this writing, there are 22 states that have passed legislation designating square dancing as the 'state folk dance.' [...] Perhaps they see these laws as a way to promote their activities. However, this strategy overlooks the negative public relations generated from a tactic that says to the rest of the dance world 'we are better than you.'"

Crawford, again with Rose, saw fit to praise each and every lazy cover shot she's ever supplied, with the exception of that used by *The Web Magazine*.

OK, maybe Cindy's dis was entirely circumstantial, but this is the web. In the context of alien autopsies, the Bavarian Illuminati, the invention of AIDS in a Minnesota lab, and all the other cockeyed notions we all ostensibly believe in, there's no such thing as inadmissible evidence. Considering that paranoia is the slander with which the web is currently being pilloried, the situation could only be more apt if Perot had taken his election campaign to web ad banners rather than television infomercials.

Then again, you showcase hara-kiri where you can find an appreciative crowd, preferably one willing to pay to see it again. Here again, television is proving itself more adept than the web, quickly morphing the traditionally dim weekend into a nut-cake smorgasbord. From Friday's first minutes of *Sliders*, the afternoon-special-like "portal into a parallel universe," to the out-there "truths" of Sunday's *X-Files*, it's obvious that the gurus of programming have taken notice of a nation of Dilberts who don't get out much on the weekends.

Nestled amidst various Profilers, Pretenders, and Millennialists, perhaps the most cynical – and inspired – moment of the weekend's new programming schedule arrived in the form of *Dark Skies*. Billed as

Kooks Museum
http://www.teleport.com/~dkossy/
For finding the complete and unexpurgated texts of the kinds of loopy tracts and pamphlets usually confined to Greyhound terminal benches, no finer resource exists online than the Kooks Museum. Curated by Donna Kossy, author of *Kooks: A Guide to the Outer Limits of Human Belief,* the virtual museum is an affectionately produced – though harsh-on-the-eyes – bullshit buffet of treatises on psychosmology, electro-alchemy, and hollow-earth theories, to name some of the more reasonable entries. Strongly recommended for those who find Fox Mulder exasperatingly skeptical.

"reality-based programming," *Dark Skies* offered a best-of-both-worlds premise, where the *Weekly World News*'s Batboy lurks in the wings of the Ed Sullivan Theater, eyeing the Beatles hungrily while awaiting orders from Roswell. The subtext of such a series is that neither bullshit nor truth alone has sustained appeal, but when combined they may at least prove good for a chuckle, if not a ratings point or two.

Which gives rise to the most deranged hypothesis of all: assuming that the networks are out to get the networked, they just might want to keep us once they have us. And the twisted media give-and-take might prove to work in ways nobody ever predicted. After all, for the web, "cesspool of groundless rumor, intrigue, and conspiracy" is a much better proposed tag line than *The New York Times*ian squib, "the graphical, multimedia portion of the Internet" could ever aspire to be. With any luck, it may even prove more vivid and tenacious than the image of a failed nominee, tumbling downward, dragging parties, platforms, and palaver along with him.

Search and Destroy

by Duke of URL

THE first web page was a résumé. The second named the first "Cool Site of the Year" and presented it with a ghastly HTML-ready award GIF. The third was a hotlist, assiduously indexing the previous two. Even if this time line isn't exactly true, it may as well be. What's undeniable is the speed at which all three archetypal web clichés have been made irrelevant. Like the droll HTML exhibitionists and the dubious coolspotters, the hotlist overextended its welcome by the entire duration of its existence, and even the most accommodating Internet grazers started to question the utility of the form. With either the same thirty sites crowding the real estate or massive directories defying decipherability, each new iteration looked less like information evolution and more like the Talmud on Miracle-Gro.

But redundancy and fecklessness alone didn't sink the hotlist – sometime between Yahoo!'s migration from *akebono.stanford.edu* to *netscape.com* servers, and sometime after the day that popularity wore down NCSA's What's New page, homepage auteurs ceased to be the librarian-arbiters of web traversability. Responsibility fell snugly into the adult undergarments of those who could afford massive parallelism – a group brewed by Lycos and curdled by Hotbot, all promising to serve up a sample of everything, everywhere, in ten-location increments. And if one ignored their escalatingly dubious and questionably implemented claims, well – for clue-surfers everywhere, it was an agreeable, if grossly overcrowded, walk in the park.

If you're a small-time web publisher whose idea of marketing is to

load 30k of euphemisms for oral sex onto the bottom of your homepage, the glut and gluttony of the search engine industry are ideal. But if the only thing going down on your leased line is quote.com's report on your Excite shares, you might have a different perspective. The former have reacted predictably to Open Text's recent announcement of its intent to sell preferred placement of well-heeled URLs on its Open Text index, calling for a boycott of the service. Short-sellers aside, the latter will be wishing Excite had jumped on the idea first.

When Internet **traditionalists** call for a boycott of the Open Text index – always one of the lesser-known members of the vast search engine crowd – they ignore the fact that it was already being boycotted, simply for always being one of the lesser-known members of the vast search engine crowd. Some are frightened that Open Text's pay-to-play move could bring a Reaganesque split in web traffic, where the rich get richer and the poor cheat on welfare. After all, it's a principal truth of the media economy that freedom of speech is superseded by the priorities of the free market, which assume anything worth saying is worth paying to

say. And, with any luck, worth paying to hear.

But then, freedom of speech is a distinct creature from equal access, a term classically employed in discussions of available and affordable service (as in access to the Playboy Channel). But just as the net elegantly solves production cost and bottleneck issues, familiar questions of distribution networks and mechanisms linger – not related to distribution of the document, but to the notice of its existence. At play is the same promotional clout that guarantees thousands of screens for the latest Disney rehash, builds Baked Lays displays at the heads of supermarket aisles, and grabs full-page real estate for pink-chip Escort Services in the A-M volume of the Yellow Pages.

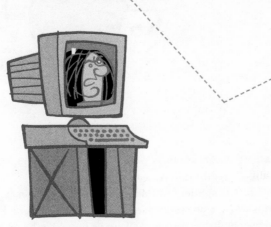

Protesting this inevitable fact of life is understandable – and those who recall the days before Usenet was smothered by spam, when commerce was anathema to the Internet, may be inclined to offer a sympathetic nod. But busting one's head out the window and playing the angry prophet, railing against the transformation from information to infomercial, will meet with as much success as Alan Keyes outside of Atlanta's WSBTV – not only barred from the debate, but dragged away with nary a blip on CNN.

As sure as a level playing field suggests a nice site for an office building, the web will continue to be pushed toward the flatline. Those who see the new world media order as a system of representation more conspicuously taxing than anything since the middle eighteenth century will likely find no Tea Party to call their own. But when *Independence Day 2* rolls out, those who were patiently waiting for a real revolution can be sure that they've already heard its call to armchairs. You'll know them by their résumés and defiant ribbons of excellence.

Murky Brown

by Duke of URL

IF information is power, then the current wave of bullshit could appropriately be termed a "brownout."

The subtlety of this axiom wasn't lost on Wall Street speculators this week, who responded to the Internet players' PR speed chess match with a bullish stance on AOL and a bearish take on Netscape – proof positive that it pays big to be fooled, as long as you're prepared to be fooled again and again, as often as possible. Assuming relevance goes hand in hand with popularity, those who studied NPD Research's PC-Meter stats on web usage, released this week, would conclude that late-breaking news has little value at all.

Working from a statistically significant but contextually archaic sample of one thousand home users, NPD Research shouldn't have been surprised that its client-side tracking software reported that the most visited sites on the web were the default homepages assigned by the current batch of online services. And if the boneheads at NPD listed *mcom.com* (Mosaic Communications, or presettlement Netscape, which ranked thirteenth in the lineup) and *netscape.com* (which ranked third) separately, who's to complain? In the study, news sites, with a 6 percent share, trailed far behind every other category, including educational, "adult" (which we like to think of as "educational"), and even government sites. Curiously, the "news" that *aol.com* was the most visited site on the web was revisited quite a few times in NPD's study and press releases.

It may be the fate of would-be information and questionable statistics to be of more and more value to fewer and fewer people. Of course,

the real winner of this infotainment lottery was NPD, whose press release also performed the neat trick of auto-stimulation by noting that the company's quarterly reports are available for the modest sum of US$50K (with an additional US$125K throwing consultation into the bargain). Still, given the tenor of the times, such data only served as a bolstering footnote to AOL's week-long promotional bowel movement, a series of nonevents that the business press, not unsurprisingly, covered like flies.

AOL, voted "Most Popular by the Web," jilts Netscape for Microsoft! AOL licenses Java! AOL commences talks with AT&T! If Michael Ovitz were involved, we'd half-expect a tiresome tell-all best seller and an HBO original movie by summer.

It only makes sense that AOL, the reigning champion of charging phenomenally for what is otherwise available for free, would turn playing coy into a cacophony. But, while **Ted Leonsis,** president of AOL, lectures on the sophistication of "disaggregation," Bill Gates puts the principle into practice, cementing the success of Microsoft in the browser market by giving MSIE to AOL, Netcom, and CompuServe, while apparently offering little more in return than a slot on the long menu of online services in Son of Windows 95.

"AOLephantiasis," by Strep Throat
http://www.suck.com/daily/96/02/26/
From "AOLephantiasis," Suck's report on the heretical commentary of Ted Leonsis, then-president of AOL Services, Co., at the TED conference:
"The future of the web is programming, and Leonsis isn't talking about CGI scripts. Competition, for AOL's Mr. Big, is anything that prevents you from logging into his service as soon as you get home. Not surprisingly, the main challenger, after spouses and children, is TV. From the big board of his control room, Leonsis and Case can watch the modem connections dropping as thousands of AOL users forego the dubious pleasures of AOL People Connection in favor of an evening with Jerry. Seinfeld is one of the only shows that puts a dent in AOL's ratings. (Interestingly, Leonsis argues that a loser in the couch-potato-versus-mouse-potato sweeps is the Cable News Network, raising the issue of whether or not AOL is now 'the white man's CNN.') At this moment, wanna-be web programmers across the country are readying their pitches: 'I see it as a combination Seinfeld and The Spot.' May we suggest Suckfeld?"

AOL bigwigs may not have "been taking stupid pills," but someone obviously slipped them some Spanish Fly – what else could explain the gang-bang merger orgy in which everyone who played got the short end of a very big stick? But their pain is nothing compared to Netscape's – Netscape loved AOL until AOL, who hated Microsoft, leveraged Microsoft's greater hate for Netscape to their advantage. Now Netscape's just hatin'.

Naturally, the news of these murky deals has a greater impact than their far-off realities. All the companies involved are hungry, and the money flows when investors see what they're hungry for, regardless of whether any of them will ever get it. Fully aware that contempt is a small price to pay for familiarity, everyone wants that all-important first hit – the desktop icon that gives the soon-to-be-familiar Internet dial tone.

Meanwhile, Clark ponders, Leonsis panders, Gates plunders, and the rest of us are left scratching our heads. The future? Armchair investing replaces the state lottery, as the news – faster, better, and more illusory – gets spun out of control. We see big dollars and their stunt-doubles crossing palms and T1 lines. We see the finest bullshit money can buy.

AOL Mulling Web Availability Of Flagship Brand
http://www.zdnet.com/intweek/daily/960306a.html
"We haven't been taking stupid pills," Leonsis told *Inter@ctive Week* reporter Steven Vonder Haar. "We're going to do what our members ask us to do, and they've been asking us to do this." Meaning "disaggregation," the separation of content from network dial-up services traditionally united under one charge on AOL. Perhaps the stupid pills were simply taking time to digest, as AOL later ceased its disaggregation plans, closed down its GNN ISP service, and, instead, offered flat-fee pricing, which only succeeded in bringing its network to its knees.

Wiping the Slate Clean

by Ann O'Tate

IT'S the principle that governs both soccer riots and internal mailing list bellyaching – schoolhouse mischief is easy if the rest of the class is doing it anyway. So we're hardly surprised that the pestiferous peal of nails scraping blackboard echoed throughout the net this week, as would-be web toughs dog-piled on the new kid on the block. The teasing started long ago – he had hardly **unpacked his bags** before the first noogie was cracked, and he was beat up regularly even before his first day.

But the vector of the vitriol aimed at Slate is off the mark – nothing more than <u>snottiness on autopilot,</u> a perverse form of initiation rivaling de-pantsing in both maturity and wit. Obviously, under normal

> **"Reinventing the Zine," by Steven Johnson (May 9, 1996)**
> http://www.feedmag.com/96.05_filter.html
> "All the evidence suggests that Michael Kinsley's uber-zine, Slate -- due on these silicon shores in mid-June – will continue Microsoft's tried-and-true corporate strategy: first, let the other guys do the real innovation, then swoop down on the market and cop all their moves."

> **"Slate Comes Out Cold," by Gary Kamiya (June 25, 1996)**
> http://www.salon1999.com/media/media2960625.html
> "Not even the most epochal of publications could have lived up to [Slate's] not-since-amoebas-crawled-from-the-primeval-ooze hype, and by the iron laws of Trendoid Journalism a revulsion against all things bright and Kinsleyesque will inevitably follow. Before donning surgical mask and gloves, therefore, we will pause for a brief moment of commiseration with our new Web colleagues. Pause. OK, nurse, hand me that chain saw." –Gary Kamiya at Salon, "Slate Comes Out Cold," shortly after Slate's launch.

circumstances, we'd be the first ones to applaud such behavior, if not the first to engage in it.

For once, we advise caution. This particular newbie may look scrawny and act befuddled, but he comes from a rich neighborhood, and he's a quick study. His coy pleonasm hides a wealth of willpower, animus, and, well, wealth – we're reminded of an arrogant but all-too-accurate college cheer (familiar to anyone whose degree cost more than many single-family homes): "That's alright, that's okay, you're going to work for us someday." If it's true that media is like the weather, then either Microsoft's put together one of the finest forecast teams ever, or it's extraordinarily adept at harnessing the wind. Either way, we're positive that it'll be Kinsley still standing after the storm subsides.

Sure, lobbing potshots through the clue gaps of Slate's decidedly unweb interface and playing "guess the research source" for its retreaded essay topics is easy and fun. And as for its much-vaunted "Does Microsoft Play Fair" roundtable – well, AltaVista could produce deeper criticism than what the gathered industry shills spouted. But those who write off Slate on the basis of this first issue are essentially putting out bug reports, not product reviews.

Microsoft's workmanlike approach to creating original content seems laughable at first. The company approaches putting out a magazine exactly as it would putting out a software package, right down to hiring the man behind Microsoft Works as "publisher" of the yet-unnamed, yet-undefined product. It's not just that Microsoft has left itself room to upgrade, but, like a word-processing package, Slate is more of a medium than a message . . . its ideological slant isn't presented so much as implied, and its utility is less that of a source than a distillation.

Given its mediumness, perhaps it's expected that online critics have taken so much pleasure in pointing out that Slate takes little "advantage" of the web. If they're referring to its unfriendly download times and radically unbrowsable navigation – well, page numbers have worked for books for a long time and, obviously, Slate on Paper is going to be how people will actually read the thing. *Slate.com* is only a detour, a distraction from the Starbuck's distribution deal, which itself is the surest guarantee of page views since Net Search.

Others have whined that Slate's editorial inattention to its own medium is the problem: there's no industry coverage, really, and the few links included are either buried or "jokes." Certainly, there's little in content or presentation that couldn't appear in the nonvirtual pages of *Newsweek* or *The New Yorker* or *The New Republic*. Indeed, most of Slate – in some form or another – already has. This is explicit in "The Week/The Spin" and "In Other Magazines" – our favorite sections – but the rest of Slate shows signs of gentle repurposing as well: "Down-sizing Downsizing" revisits a *New Yorker* piece from March, the Miss Manners review covers the same territory as *Spy's* recent Martha Stewart exposé, and "A Bad End" is a Roget-aided rewrite of a month-old *Entertainment Weekly* wrap-up.

We happen to think this is a strategy (not shovelware so much as studied garbagology) that will work. Kinsley and company are selling high-brow cultural Cliff's Notes, and the proposed twenty-dollar subscription fee is cheap compared to the time you might spend keeping up otherwise. Some argue that Kinsley siphoned style and approach from Salon, but Slate appears to be a website for people who *don't* read. People like us.

Indeed, we may be suffering from a fit of solipsism, but we actually find much of ourselves in Slate. Aside from our shared aversion to our shared medium, there's a deeper resonance – an arch dismissal of common sense, an eagerness to beat a dead horse until we rouse its ghost. Where we part is only in our methods.

The situation has an unlikely analog within the pages of Slate itself – an anecdote in David O. Russell's diary:

"Chip Brown's dinner party last night. There's a really successful cardio-surgeon there who also happens to be very handsome. The combination is enough to make you want to punch the guy. But he turns out to be a nice guy. Which is another reason to punch him. We debate methods for changing our children's poopie diapers, and I am advocating the bare hand method (with warm water at the sink) versus the aloe-loaded wet wipes . . . [the discussion eventually] leads to his declaration that toilet paper gives you hemorrhoids, that it's better to use your hand."

Well, of course it is – and if this tale is anything to go by, Slate will be coming around soon.

Ex Libris

by Dilettante

"Meditating on the Library as Archive: From Alexandria to the Internet," by Daniel Rubey
http://math240.lehman.cuny.edu/talkback/ Talk_html/CenterP-Rubey-1-capt.html
"The archetypal Library of Alexandria is an emblem of knowledge lost, a site where the avatars of the future destroyed the texts of the classical past. Built by Ptolemy in the third century B.C. from the worm-eaten fragments of Aristotle's library, the Alexandrian library was partly destroyed in 47 B.C. when fire spread from Julius Caesar's ships ablaze in the harbor. It was further damaged by Aurelian in 272, and finally demolished by Emporer Theodosius's Christians in an anti-paganism riot in 391. Twelfth-century Christians rewrote this history as an apocryphal account of the Arab General Amr destroying the library out of Koranic zeal."

IN ancient times – say, before the Arpanet – libraries were occasionally destroyed along with the rest of a building, a city, or a culture. These charmingly unambiguous accomplishments of our ancestors provide a historical motif that we can instantly recognize and reflexively deplore. True, some are probably grateful to have been spared another semester's worth of soporific classics, but on average society still considers the book burners the bad guys. In our postliterate age, the main danger to libraries is not marauding Huns but perceived obsolescence, the notion that libraries are quaint and elitist, sort of like classical music and the daily paper. The Internet, in some fat-pipe dream of universal access, will relieve us of the burden of research in the same way that television relieved us of reading for news and entertainment.

The fantasy of being digital insists that information is only as good as the methods available to search for it. Online information rules here, since it can be referenced in previously unimaginable ways: by geography, by heuristically determined literary style, by quality of pornographic content. The reductio ad absurdum of this idea is the so-called intelligent agent, a vessel in which, to paraphrase Jaron Lanier, we can dilute our personality, a device that will ultimately allow the information that we want to come looking for us. In the plot of this just-so story each host on the net is another monkey typing, and at the happy conclusion the agent brings us Shakespeare.

It would be difficult to argue that searching for information on the Internet is inconvenient. Already many people look to the web before any other information source, and therein lies the problem. Even if you can reduce the ten thousand hits gained via AltaVista down to a handful, a really good source must be both authentic and permanent, or, as computer scientists would say, "persistent."

The design of the Internet and the web is ideal for exchanging ephemeral data between trusted parties. Net experts will argue that authenticity can be ensured on the Internet using PGP-like schemes, but this provides only technical trust and doesn't account for the shared confidence that most people mean by "authenticity." On the Internet, it seems that consensus has been found by the infra-left and the ultra-right ("**We are all puppets controlled by unseen masters**"); but the visible portion of the political spectrum only manages a confusing pluralism that mirrors society at large. Which isn't surprising – this is a culture

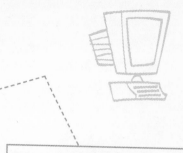

VALS Segmentation System
http://future.sri.com/vals/dframe/dia3.html
Are you experienced? If you subscribe to *Penthouse, EW, GQ,* or *Hot Rod* (not the porno mag), you may well be, if only technically. Stanford Research Institute's VALS Segmentation System is a method for plugging people into categories defined by "values and lifestyles," such as Experiences, as in the above case. Whether you conform to the stereotypes is, naturally, up to you, but that won't stop enterprising marketers from punching your ticket. And if you really don't fit into the VALS breakdown of motivation driven by principle, status, or action, you're probably dead – and dead men bear no sales.

where we can see *Beavis and Butt-head* and *Portrait of a Lady* at the same cineplex, and no one is too surprised if it's the Henry James fans who wear Metallica T-shirts and slurp jumbo Cokes. God only knows what might get by the Internet's drain trap and settle into respectable thought.

Libraries at least serve as a cultural band-pass filter, an imperfect but workable way to salvage some signal from a flood of noise. Traditional libraries, though they may be inefficient and bureaucratic by the standards of the Internet, are more than book repositories. They are a naive sanctification of knowledge, manifesting the hopeful belief that high ceilings and artificial solemnity will bestow credibility. As for permanence,

books may be stolen, destroyed, lost, or misfiled; but they seldom change their own content and they're usually stored in a format that people can still read ten years after publication. When information does become mostly electronic, maintaining it will require elaborately conceived digital libraries. David Levy and Catherine Marshall of Xerox PARC, who design such things, understated it nicely: the Internet's infrastructure "lacks the crucial institutional services, such as collection development and cataloging, by which collections are stabilized for ongoing use." Even a congressional subcommittee could determine that current libraries do this job pretty well.

If all knowledge really were power, or even a direct antecedent, no one would question the relevance of libraries. Rather, we'd insist upon – and probably pay for – these sources of information. But much of what libraries hold, especially basic research, has a deferred value that engenders a justifiable, if unfortunate, lack of exploitation. The Internet, though, passed the peak of its scruples back when the government discovered that it had accidentally created something useful. When the well-heeled invent a mechanism for buying preferred packets like they do first-class airline seats, the economy section will get light-headed from sucking bits through a narrow straw. It will be a bad time to find that the city library has been converted to a parking garage.

POLITICALLY iNCOHERENT

In the past, attitudes toward world and national leaders were defined by particular sets of events, by the lucky congruence of media and message into History. Roosevelt's post–Pearl Harbor address. The McCarthy Trial. The launch of Sputnik. The Zapruder film. Nixon's resignation. For us, the combination of cable news' sleepless hunger for footage and the parallel evolution of policy into infinitely divisible announcements – each as targeted as a new cola launch, though few as successfully positioned – has transformed politics from a quadrennial two-

ring circus (with the occasional sideshow) into a twenty-four-hour video arcade.

Seen in this light – the flickering blue of a cathode tube – you can begin to understand that John Hinkley, Jr. gave us the first tangible demonstration of media interactivity. A marriage of pop obsession and political activism, Hinkley's futile fixation confirmed for a new generation the equivalence of show business and politics even as he gave indirect evidence as to the impotence of individual action in the age of mega-PACs and soft money.

Weaned on consumerist metaphors designed to convince us that time is money and that ideological disputes can be settled by comparison shopping in "the marketplace of ideas," we chose, when it comes to elections, to take our business elsewhere. Commentators who damn young people's reluctance to participate in the persistent myth of democracy miss the upside of our renegotiated social contract. We understand with a savvy born of both *Sesame Street* and Rush Limbaugh just how inseparable politics is from our daily lives, that even refusing to vote won't exclude us from the process – inexplicably huge, incomprehensibly tangled.

Politics on the personal level is the subject of E. L. Skinner's "Enlightened Self-Disinterest," and of Justine's rules for those crossing political boundaries in search of a date, "Sex and the Single URL." On a grander scale, "The Third Time as 'Tragedy'" comments on the relative merits of Capulets and Clintons and marvels at the perennial appeal of revolution as both term-limit and plot device. More traditional political commentary is itself the subject of "Master of Ceremony," a stinging, hilariously hurtful barb in the fleshy side of presidential debate moderator Jim Lehrer.

As long as the media persists in covering political contests like horse races, the fact that we're not waving betting tickets at the finish line will seem like a statement of indifference. But if we weren't paying attention, we wouldn't be able to laugh. Politics is a sit-com, albeit one whose ratings would place it somewhere between the seventh season of *Who's the Boss* and *After M*A*S*H*. What's needed is a way to translate the perhaps unintended acuity of our jocular analysis into a language that politicians themselves can understand. After all, for an ailing body politic, laughter is the best medicine, or at least the most readily available anesthetic. Mao Tse-tung may have been right that "political power grows out of the barrel of a gun," but little did he know how big a fish would be sitting at the other end.

Enlightened Self-Disinterest

by E. L. Skinner

Thomas Malthus

http://www.ucmp.berkeley.edu/history/malthus.html

While E. L. Skinner name-checks eighteenth century political economist Thomas Malthus only to underscore libertarians' helpful contribution to the ongoing process of natural selection, it's difficult to ignore the applicability of his theories on population to the state of the web today: massive growth followed by epidemic outbreaks of famine and disease. In this regard, Suck's daily dose of pestilence is only a modest proposal.

AS IF the ghost of Malthus were coming back to haunt us in our pending overpopulation, libertarians may be giving us the evolutionary kick in the ass we need to get natural selection dusted off and chugging along again. On nearly every consumer front, civil libertarians stand poised, ready to off themselves in the interest of almighty personal rights. Indeed, Uncle Sam appears to have bought himself a clue after the *Wheel of Fortune* landed on Oklahoma City last year. Flag-burning survivalists and code-crunching anarchists everywhere should be pleased as punch. The Fed is finally backing off and letting you do all the things you've been dying to do to yourself. And not a moment too soon, really.

Aspartame – which is to NutraSweet what photocopies are to Xerox – recently became a raison d'être among beverage-rights activists. Seems a study by Washington University discovered a substantial increase in the incidence of brain tumors nationwide during the last ten years, the period in which Nutrasweet knocked off saccharin as the dieter's perfectly legal carcinogen of choice. In the meantime, Aspartame has become as American as Mom, Apple Pie, and Fresca. Judging from the FDA's cool response to the findings, the fact that it might give you brain cancer shouldn't really be cause for concern. Besides, we wouldn't want to interfere with your God-given right to lose weight. Go ahead: kick back and crack another Diet Coke. Have some Olestra-dipped chips while you're at it. Americans' willingness to defer pain for short-term gain (er, loss) brings to mind a graffito rumored to

Kill Yourself

http://www.justnet.com.sg/KY/purpose.html

As emphatic as it is muddled, Kill Yourself e-zine exemplifies what happens when people confuse adolescent rebellion with political activism. Kill Yourself's laundry list of what's "wrong with the world today" includes "the mainstream, education, the government, religion, [and] ignorance." The further addition of America and "Earth" makes one wonder what exactly might be left for "etc., etc." to cover. The editor's touchingly confused disavowal of responsibility – admitting on the one hand that "we all know what the problems are but we're too lazy to offer solutions" and then stating that "all that matters is the free distribution of information" – seems equally indicative of '90s political activism, where the corollary of "Do It Yourself" is "Because No One Else Will Do It For You."

OUR HERO

New Zealand Infotech Weekly
(November 4, 1996)

http://www.infotech.co.nz/november_4/nxedu.html

New Zealand's *Infotech Weekly* reports on how a group of Motor City teens used a collection of scanned cover art and ludicrously overheated "gangsta" slang to dupe much of the mainstream press into thinking that a street gang (the "Glock 3," who at last call were still hangin' at *www.glock3.com*) had invaded cyberspace. It took one of the net's own, Cyberwire Dispatch's Brock Meeks, to pop a cap on the group's hoax. An object lesson in the press's willingness to believe the worst about the net and urban youth, especially in combination, the fiasco shows that old media's complaints about the absence of new media fact-checking runs both ways. Meeks's report cleared up most of the errors in regards to "Glock 3," but to call the ruse "the world's first 'cyber media prank,'" only means he wasn't paying attention when Suck launched.

The Barbra Streisand Memorabilia Museum

http://mgfx.com/barbra/

Sadly, the Barbra Streisand Museum is for real.

have graced the guillotine: "Lose ten pounds of useless fat – instantly!"

Such apocalyptic truths are apparent not just under the knife, but behind the wheel. Not wanting the FDA to monopolize rule-bending in the federal rumpus room, the National Highway Traffic Safety Administration announced it will allow car owners to disconnect the air bags in their cars. This comes as the result of growing concern – some would say hysteria – that the safety devices occasionally injure or kill motorists. (Apparently a much more terrifying way to go than slamming into the steering column or punching through the windshield.) Given the fact that around thirty people have been killed by the forceful expulsion of an air bag against some thirteen hundred who've been saved, it's a little like keeping your gun loaded all the time because you'd prefer not to be pistol-whipped to death.

Guns, of course, have been a long-standing icon of inalienable and irrelevant rights. God knows, you never can tell when we might need to scramble the well-regulated militia against domestic enemies like crack babies, **gangsta rappers,** or Barbra Streisand. Notwithstanding the recent image problems of the NRA, we feel comfortable in saying that our forefathers would be horrified if they knew deer populations threatened to overrun the countryside, and rural stop signs stood for decades without being plugged by a .20 gauge. We figure these incidents wouldn't occur if local yokels were bending their elbows instead of pumping lead: forget handgun laws and assault rifle bans – what we really need is a unilateral elimination of blue laws.

The deregulation of alcohol might help facilitate a whole range of libertarian civil programs and social causes. Why, just last month the Institute of Medicine discovered that 12 million cases of sexually transmitted disease are diagnosed every year in the United States, not a few of them the result of carousing after the bar closes. On the other hand, a

University of California study found that smoking cigarettes significantly sharpens short-term learning and memory. Now, if we could just get people to smoke before they have sex so they remember how and why to use a condom – it'd be a solution of Solomonic proportions.

It all goes to show you that the net and the PC are wimpy second-stringers in the critical fight for civil liberties. Indeed, alcohol, tobacco, and firearms are the triumvirate of the libertarian vanguard, and the jackbooted ATF is its arch enemy. Now if we could just finalize the medical use of pot, consummate it with freedom from motorcycle helmets, and seal it with a needle exchange, we might have a real positive impact on the workplace. Like drastically increasing the morbidity of middle management and other paranoid survivalists in bunkers from Missoula to Mountain View.

Anheuser-Busch's Position on Alcohol and the Shooting Sports
http://www.budweiser.com/huntsafe.html
It's good to read that the folks at *Budweiser.com* would like to remind Bud drinkers who hunt that "alcohol can affect his or her skills." We can't help but notice the reluctance to specify the effect as positive or negative, and since elsewhere Budweiser strives to convince us that its brew will make one better looking, better feeling, and, well, just plain better, we wonder why it is we're supposed to wait until after the shoot to drink, especially since it helps us score everywhere else.

The Third Time as "Tragedy"

by Dr. McLoo

GOOD morning – or, as Leonardo DiCaprio prefers, "Good morrow." Do you still feel guilty for not voting? As local citizens flocked ovinely to the polls, cutting short hurried breakfasts to drop another polite turd on the statistical dungheap, more than a few web wiseacres took the opportunity for a cheap laugh or a bitter jibe. As a few helpful English lads told us last spring, "voting is pointless, humanity has evolved beyond the point of democracy," etc. Or, as Louis Rossetto put it recently: "People believe electoral politics is democracy because they have been brainwashed, period."

Me, I voted! But I have to admit the process lacked drama. Where's the thrill in voting compared to, say, storming the Bastille? Isn't there supposed to be a revolution going on?

Oh, you were talking about a digital revolution? Well, still.

I fear that in this one rare instance our friends the anarcholibertarian revolutionaries may be misled. Humanity has not evolved beyond the point of democracy. Voting is not pointless. Voting has a very definite point. The point of voting is to build traffic. Go ahead. Help Dave and Buster out.

But let's think for a second about that sense of disappointment. Wouldn't a nice little social cataclysm have livened things up? It is not just the Tofflers et al. who thrill to the sound of some third wave crashing down. The hope for a bitter end and for the looted luxuries of revolution suffused the fat fall *Vogue*, in which, among the photographs of clothing inspired by military officers and by the Empire's stylish beneficiaries of the tumbrel, we read that photographer François Halard keeps a Sevres cast of Marie Antoinette's breast on his mantle, next to a Twombly print.

The familiar rhetoric of revolution has a history of gentrification, of course. Right-wingers wield it with self-congratulatory irony, and our highly regarded colleagues in the digital garrets of the '90s (not sans-culottes, certainly, but with a definite preference for shorts) use it to garrote the more traditional fourth estate. And just at the moment when these revolutionary cries rise and then seem to die disappointingly away, the peculiar golden colors of an imaginary revolutionary aftermath begin to appear in fashion advertisements and in movies inspired by fashion advertisements.

For instance, on the shores of Verona Beach, Leonardo DiCaprio (*Premiere* calls him "D," his cute set nickname) and his Montague homies twirl their guns and wait for the vile Capulets to show. Baz Luhrmann's Verona is postapocalyptic, but this is no *Blade Runner*. The waves lap seductively, the boys and girls wear pretty clothes, and Camille Paglia would be pleased to note that people dance and shoot at each other as a form of joyful sport. And despite the ending, when Juliet puts a bullet through her head surrounded by hundreds of lit candles, what you have here, mainly, is a happy apocalypse.

I'm all in favor. We all know already that the cries of faux-rebellion are linked in fantasy not to the terrors they articulate but to the unspoken wish for and anticipation of a restoration of order – and not even with a different gang on top, though maybe with a few new members. That's the harmless rhetorical fun of it.

Sometimes, though, I worry. If the wonderful Luhrmann missed the

Talkin' Bout Our G-G-G-Generation
http://www.vivid.com/culture/coolthings .html#garb
Website developers Vivid put up this guide to becoming one of the "web generation" sometime after *Rolling Stone* wrote about the weekly geek potluck known as "Thursday Night Dinner" and before the bungled Wired IPO and the *Rolling Stone* story on "geeksploitation." The web's version of *The Preppy Handbook*.

Familyville's Voting Booth
http://www.familyville.com/intro/vote/msn/
One of the less noxious of the net's bald-faced ploys for click-throughs (annual attempts at which go by such names as "The Webbies" and "The Digital Hollywood Awards"), no doubt is due to the fact that its organizers seem genuinely interested in whether or not you like the Windows or Mac operating system best. Proof that all politics is still local, though: as a "family site" run by a Christian group, Familyville eschews the standard construction when asking the reader to vote on the man netizens love to hate, jettisoning "Is Bill Gates the Anti-Christ?" in favor of the more conservative "Is Bill Gates Big Brother?"

"There's No Government Like No Government: An Interview of Louis Rossetto," by David Hudson
http://www.sfbg.com/Live/cyber/interview.html
The similarities between Wired Ventures' resident visionary, Louis Rossetto, and Russian anarchist Mikhail Bakunin begin and end with the belief that, to quote Bakunin, "the State is the organized authority, domination, and power of the possessing classes over the masses the most complete negation of humanity." The proof of Rossetto's stylish anarchism (and equally stylish rejection of Bakunin's other arguments) lies in this interview. Highlights include Rossetto's skillful juggling of several digerati catchphrases into a single textual . . . er, spew:
"This new world is characterized by a new global economy which is inherently anti-hierarchical and decentralist . . . [it's] not about top down control to accomplish either selfish or noble ends, but about a global hive mind that is arriving at a new, spontaneous order. . . . Wired is not about regurgitating nineteenth century social thinking. . . . Wired is about talking about this erupting future."

point, and presented Romeo and Juliet as innocent victims rather than as crazy kids drunk on rhetoric who didn't know when to stop, might our friends and colleagues make the same mistake? Will the **Bryant Street Bakunians and digital revolutionaries** you find theorizing in South Park and Silicon Alley actually poison themselves on resentment? After delivering their lines, will they fail to snap out of it?

"I've completely embraced the concept of 'tragedy,'" said Claire Danes recently to *W*, leaving readers to wonder whether the actress's intonation or the irony of New York copy editors had added the quotation marks. Still, right on, Claire. Here in the land of digital politics, we've completely embraced the concept of "revolution."

But God protect us and the mansions of our masters from "a universal rebellion on the part of the people." Like the porcelain-breasted Antoinette and her indecisive husband, they don't really have a taste for violence. Shooting and looting make them nervous.

This suggests a business opportunity. The Palo Alto papers have been advertising etiquette classes for high-tech companies whose engineers and executives don't know how to hold a fork. The next step: bejeweled armaments, such as long swords and flamethrowers, plus classes on how to handle them, for our friends who want to take their fantasies to the next level. The ultimate in digital edutainment: shooting the pike from the hands of a knave at the head of a mob in Sunnyvale.

Master of Ceremony

by LeTeXan

THE presidential debates are a story we tell ourselves about ourselves: we're a deeply intellectual, issue-oriented, content-rich, free, democratic society that wants nothing more than . . . yawn . . . pass the Fritos and the PlayStation.

Wouldn't you rather be watching a cockfight? Anthropological analysis can make even a cockfight bloodless – metaphorically speaking, of course. Under the microscope of Clifford Geertz, a cockfight isn't meaty, it's meta. And this despite (or perhaps because of) the ceremony's having had its "practical consequences removed and reduced . . . to the level of sheer appearances."

In the most recent presidential instance, however, we weren't faced with "a chicken hacking another mindlessly to bits"; instead, it was more like a contest between two piano-playing chickens in a fairground vending machine, the winner decided by who pecked out the more convincingly appealing version of our favorite political tunes.

So it hardly matters whether you liked Bob Dole's edgy, carping version of "So What Cha Want?" or Bill Clinton's sonorous, wonkish rendition of "What You Got" (including a plaintive chorus of "Baby, Baby, Baby, Gimme One More Chance!"). The stupefying sameness of the debate after its first 90/60/30 exchange led us to realize that chickens will always be chickens: they strut and preen and have sharp, pointed beaks – instruments largely unsuited to articulating policy visions, but highly useful when pecking PAC pockets for advertising scratch. What was most telling, then, was not the shrill, chattering debate machine, but the

man chosen to pump it full of quarters. Who was that ask-man?

Why Jim Lehrer, of course, host of the *NewsHour* on PBS and reportedly the only name floated by both camps. It is telling that during protracted negotiations over knotty issues like dates, format, and dais height, the one issue both sides could agree on was moderation.

Comically overrouged and sporting more dye in his hair than even Bob Dole, the sixty-two-year-old Lehrer was the perfect choice for a major television nonevent intended to stroke the nation's collective ego. Lehrer was an avuncular, collegial, and ever-so-slightly journalistic presence nonpareil, and he deserves much of the credit for making the presidential debate series what it was: a meandering mush, a free-form duophony of prepackaged talking points and half-hearted sucker punches, barely worthy of notice and not even quite up to the nettling sound-and-fury level of a *NewsHour* panel discussion.

Lehrer's career has been an interesting and slightly tragic one, a life which mirrors in many respects the decline in fortune of one of our favorite moribund technologies, **"public" broadcasting.**

Twenty-six years ago, Lehrer, a talented city editor for the now-defunct *Dallas Times Herald*, was invited by KERA-TV to participate in an experimental roundtable program called Newsroom. In an era well

before a hydra-headed News Corp. and her Gorgon alter ego, Turner Broadcasting, *Newsroom* contained an element of seat-of-the-pants media criticism. In fact, sincere adherence to "public service" missions back then led even the local ABC affiliate in Dallas – WFAA-TV, a station owned, along with the *Dallas Morning News*, by newly inducted corporate cephalopod Belo Broadcasting – to put its homely curmudgeon of a general manager, Mike Shapiro, on the air once a week for a viewer-mail show called *Let Me Speak to the Manager*.

Such idealistic beginnings! Inside of three years, Lehrer was in Washington, D.C., flush with Fred Friendly's Ford Foundation money and teamed with Robert MacNeil to produce national public-affairs programming, including gavel-to-gavel coverage of the Watergate hearings. Lehrer has admitted that he was, at first, a bit out of his depth: in a 1992 C-SPAN interview, he described how it took stern words from the more suave and telegenic MacNeil for him to learn to stop rocking his head

back and forth, saucer-eyed, while reading the TelePrompTer. Still, at the time the very idea of "public" television was considered so "dangerous" that the Corporation for Public Broadcasting was formed to insulate individual member stations (as well as programs like MacNeil/Lehrer) from political pressure.

But now look how far he's fallen, this Icarus of Insiders. John Malone's Liberty Media, a subsidiary of TCI, now owns controlling interest in MacNeil/Lehrer Productions and thus the *NewsHour*. (Perhaps it's merely to gain easier access for his **intended drive-by on Reed Hundt**.) And instead of aggressive, idealistic reporters eager to serve the public trust, Lehrer is surrounded by the likes of Mark Shields, who receives (as Fairness and Accuracy in Reporting noted in 1995) a weekly paycheck from Lockheed Martin – the nation's largest military contractor – for his appearances on WMAL-AM's *Look at Today* radio program. Given the lingering possibility that the CPB will be "zeroed out," Lehrer may even

HotWired Hotflash (June 1994)
http://www.hotwired.com/Lib/HotFlash/ 1.08.html
"According to the Washington Post and USA Today, John Malone, the chief executive officer of Tele-Communications Inc. of Colorado, had apologized to FCC chairman Reed Hundt for saying in a Wired 2.07 interview (the July 1994 issue) that the chairman should be shot for his advocacy of new cable price controls. On Tuesday June 14, both papers reported that Malone personally called Hundt to apologize for the quote: 'All we need is a little help. . . . You know, shoot Hundt! Don't let him do any more damage.'
"As of Monday, Hundt declined to comment on the matter."

find himself privatized and back at work for Gannett or Time Warner.

So maybe it's no wonder, really, that Jim Lehrer was chosen to spend three evenings tossing whiffleballs at the candidates, or, in this last instance, helping those of others over the plate. Maybe it's to be expected that he didn't ask pointed questions about specific issues like telecom reform, or about major media donations (Seagram/MCA, Disney, Dreamworks, Time Warner, Ticketmaster) to both men's political campaigns. Even Lehrer's attempt to lure Dole into bullying Clinton on the character issue had all the subtlety of Porky Pig propping up an orange crate with a stick and a string tied to it. Lehrer long ago stopped reporting the news, and instead now passively "moderates" a flow of unquestioned political press releases.

Apparently, **no one knows the difference.** Wednesday's debate resembled less a "town-hall meeting" than a Ricki Lake set, with Lehrer in a space-age swivel desk presiding over a ghoulish parade of citizen-impersonators, whose questions belied the criticism that major media is out of touch with citizenry. Given the chance to get in the ring ourselves, it seems, we all behave a little like chickens.

The New Times York

http://c3f.com/nty1017.html

From the page formerly known as *The New Times York* (recent legal troubles have prompted a rechristening as *The Street Wall Journal;* perhaps Dow Jones can take a joke) comes the debate coverage they didn't want you to see. "Obscenities Fly at Final Debate" details Clinton and Dole's use of increasingly graphic language and gestures before coming to agree one final issue: "F*ck the soccer moms."

Sex and the Single URL

by Justine

OK, SO you've exchanged smoky glances at a CFP bar BOF. Mutual friends forwarded an absolutely adorable post he made to one of the cypherpunk lists. And he sent you a deliciously inviting postcard from his favorite impoverished Caribbean island, where he hopes to set up an anonymous-remailer offshore banking paradise! So what do you do to tease, please, and capture the heart of your technolibertarian?

Use these easy-to-follow hints and you, too, may find yourself one Sunday afternoon cuddling by a roaring fire in a Pescadero cabin, talking about digital cash! After all, there's nothing wrong with a modern girl exchanging PGP keys on a first date with the right anarchocapitalist!

Fashion tips:

DO wear your "This Shirt is a Munition" RSA T-shirt.

DON'T wear your "Solidarity Forever UPIU/AIW Local 837 Lock-Out" T-shirt.

Accessories/props:

DO have on your coffee table the original, green-cover edition of *Bionomics;* hardcover edition of *Out of Control; Crossing the Chasm;* photocopy of *True Names;* an original French-language issue of *Barbarella;* the Re/Search *Modern Primitives* issue; the *Economist* with your subscriber label discreetly visible; a 1985 issue of *Reason* (to show you are an early adopter); fund-raising appeal from The Progress and Freedom Foundation.

DON'T have on your coffee table *Savage Inequalities; Which Side Are You On; Resisting the Virtual Life; Why Things Bite Back; The New York Review of Books; Sierra; Z; Paris Review;* any novel that's not science fiction or a technothriller; fundraising appeal from the Silicon Valley Toxics Coalition.

Conversation:

DO mention how your life was changed forever when you first read Ayn Rand in eleventh grade. DO say that you think all relationships are contractual, even romantic ones. DO say that you find him so sexy that you can imagine that all the netchicks on alt.polyamory would want him. DO mention your fling with the astrophysics professor. DO say that FDR was the worst president this country ever had. DO drop these names: Friedrich Hayek; Robert Heinlein; George Gilder; David Chaum; Terence McKenna; Tom Ray; Hans Moravec; George Mason University. DO use these conversation starters: intelligent agents; sovereignty of cyber-space self-organization.

DON'T mention your fling with the liberal FCC commissioner. DON'T talk about your internship with CALPIRG. DON'T tell him that at one point you were considering a career as an art therapist. DON'T tell him about your best friend, the urban planner, who uses HUD money to develop low-income housing. DON'T mention Lyndon LaRouche. DON'T drop these names: Ben Bagdikian, Upton Sinclair, Bertolt Brecht, Barbara Ehrenreich, Carol Gilligan, Rachel Carson, Noam Chomsky, the EPA. DON'T use these conversation killers: the forty-year decline in cor-porate taxation; stockholder lawsuits; CEO compensation packages; *maquilladoras;* vulnerability. And if you really don't want to spend next Saturday night alone with your cat Patches, absolutely DON'T mention OSHA. And don't EVER catch yourself using the phrase "I can just tell, and no, I can't explain how I know it."

At any dinner party you organize for the two of you:

DO make sure there is at least one person present who a) has actually been inside the NSA; or b) owns founder's stock in a company that has held its value for more than a year after it went public; or c) has close ties with a venture capitalist.

DON'T invite anyone who a) has worked in any Democratic Party political campaign; or b) would ever use the words *multicultural* or *diversity* in a sentence, without irony; or c) does volunteer work, especially for the homeless.

Where to go and what to do:

DO plan a dream date which might include any two of the following: United Taxpayers Association luau; Digital Liberty potluck; Software Forum ice cream social; Freedom Forum rave; dinner at the Lion and Compass Lecture at the Churchill Club; browsing in the nanotechnology section at Kepler's.

DO act enthusiastic when he wants to take you to a kicky Extropian party in the Santa Cruz mountains, even if you feel like you will scream if you hear the phrases "command and control" and "cryptographic algorithm" one more time. After all, what makes him such a dear are his kooky economic models and his insane paranoia about the government – any government. And DON'T pout if he starts talking about black helicopters. Again.

DON'T sulk if he wants to make that romantic vacation you were planning as a sojourn at HOHOCON or DEFCON; DO think of it as a chance for your man to show you off to the minimum of twelve guys per square foot that will surround your every move. Let him be proud of you. Girl, this is your chance to strut your stuff with that cute leather outfit you ordered from Stormy Leather to wear just for him. DON'T suggest attending a Sunday morning service at Glide Memorial Church. DON'T take him to the Berkeley Rose Garden, which was built by the WPA. DON'T take him to a production of Ibsen's *An Enemy of the People*.

Follow these tips and see if your man doesn't let you choose what to do for your next date if you oh-so-casually let it slip that it's that divine Philip K. Dick you wish you could have met when he was still alive, instead of talking about your regret about not going up to Doris Lessing when you heard her speak at the Edinburgh Fringe.

How to tell when he is getting serious:

HE shares his best tax-evasion schemes with you. After all, what better way to start the nest egg for both of your futures than with money snatched from the tyranny and enslavement of Washington! HE says that you're the kind of girl that he would consider, if he were into contractual cohabitation.

DOs:
http://www.bionomics.org/
http://www.cfp.org/
http://www.pgp.com/
http://www.absolutkelly.com/
http://www.reason.org/

DON'Ts:
http://www.iww.org
http://www.motherjones.com
http://www.lbbs.org/zmag/index.htm
http://www.worldmedia.com/archive/
http://www.osha.gov

AD ABOUT YOU

For conspiracy theorists
who feel that the complexities
of the Trilateral Commission are beyond their grasp, the consumerist cabal unmasked by American Demographics' bottom-line approach to trends personal and professional offers a more manageable, and equally paranoid, worldview. It's an environment where breast cancer provides the jumping-off point for a Rite-Aid promotion ("We do marketing for [health-care] providers who can't.") and multiculturalism is embraced as a method for multiplying market segments ("Ethnic whites are good customers. They work hard, play hard, and spend hard.")

To be sure, the perspective of any trade magazine can be somewhat alarming – a detour into a twilight zone as eerily fixated as any John Birch meeting or Trekkies convention. The willful near-sightedness of those who claim to reveal the workings of machinery we didn't even know existed is funny only if we recognize that the guy working the control panel is as befuddled by his gear as we are. We can only laugh at the man behind the curtain if we recognize him to be the relatively powerless human being that he usually is; for many cultural critics who examine advertising, however, pushing aside the curtain does nothing to lessen the impression that one is dealing with the great and powerful Oz.

We get a similarly foreign feel from science fiction fanzines, militia newsletters, and *Supermarket News* because they all hold up a funhouse mirror to our shared culture, showing us an angle on the familiar that focuses on a part of society's anatomy we either take for granted or try to ignore. The headlines in *American Sweeper,* "The Voice of the U.S. Power Sweeping Industry" – "Then and Now" (presumably a look at, er, the sweeping changes that may banish the push broom to the dustbin of history), "The Importance of Keeping Business Parking Areas Clean" – seem touchingly provincial. Those in *Mortuary Management* – "Beware the Baby Boomers," "One Size Fits All" – strike us as morbidly fastidious. And the attempt by the *North American Actuarial Journal* to ride Gwyneth Paltrow's bustle into the mainstream – "Actuarial Issues in the Novels of Jane Austen" (assessing the accuracy of her characters' estimations of life expectancy and annuity calculations) – is endearingly geeky. For the publishers of these magazines, hyperfocus is a professional hazard. From the perspective of hammer-happy *American Builder,* everything really does look like a nail.

It's all pretty funny, if a bit uncomfortably so. Poking fun at their obsessiveness amuses us as long as we convince ourselves that these magazines' circular logic, while intersecting our lives, is closed off from them – just part of the backstage janitorial work that has to take place for us to get our gutters clean or our dead buried. Still, the cheap laugh we get from the distorted shape of American culture as hewed by someone with a very particular ax to grind has a hidden price: we never see it the same way again ourselves.

It's the permanent corrosiveness of these trade-centric visions that makes *American Demographics* such a dangerous tool in the hands of the amateur social scientist. That, and the fact that while other magazines skew editorial in favor of their particular niche, the niche of *American Demographics* is niches themselves, and the trade that AD trades in is us.

Scale is what separates the crank from the critic in this

case. The guy counting stitches in the padded walls downstate thinks there's an entire industry devoted to studying *him.* The columnists at *Adbusters,* the editors of *The Baffler,* the lay conspiracists that populate coffee shops and record stores – they know the object of study is *everyone.* The father of modern marketing wouldn't be surprised by the public's growing belief that our consumer choices and – here the marketers are more than happy to agree – therefore our very identities are wholly governed by advertising. It is the ultimate Big Lie.

Of course, believing in marketers' infallibility means ignoring their fuckups, an amnesia which might make us forget, as the Duke of URL points out in "OK Marketing," that "in the master/slave game of consumerism, we consumers are the ones holding the whip, whether we like it or not." Our reluctance to take responsibility for the scar tissue that mars consumerism's plastic face is understandable, though, as it would mean blaming ourselves for ill-conceived blights of fancy like theme restaurants. As it is, Ann O'Tate writes in "All the World's a Stage," only the lack of things to fill them prevents the infinite expansion of these architectural thyroid cases. The lacuna could be thought of as a "prop gap" measure.

Perversely, it's less discomforting to think of our relationship to advertising as Pavlovian, or, at best, codependent. In fact, sometimes it's not the object but the marketing of it that we desire. The "reasons for coming back are not the product itself, but instead the promotions and events" around it, writes Polly Esther in "Mission: Implausible," "sort of like going to the prom dateless, just for the petit fours." That a marketing campaign can sometimes make an unappetizing thing more appetizing is no surprise – take the nationwide push for lacto-tolerance as described by E. L. Skinner in "Milking It." More interesting perhaps is the idea that the unappetizing could be used to sell the already digested – see the Duke of URL detail the advertising food chain down to its septic depths, in "The Writing's on the Stall."

We want to believe that we're prisoners of Nike-Town, when in fact the totalizing vision of megamarketing could liberate us from both the tyranny of the state and apolitical boredom. Come on, "which of the following institutions evoke the strongest feelings of ardor these days: Nike, Starbucks, and Nintendo, or Congress, the Executive Office, and the FBI?" St. Huck asks us to admit in "NikeTown Crier." "There's certainly no one building fan pages for Louis Freeh."

Marketing is the preferred conspiracy theory of consumer culture, and one for which even the most hardened skeptic has a soft spot, because, like all the great conspiracies, it grows in the fertile soil of distrust, and spiraling cynicism provides its trellis. The conspirators want you to believe, and the more you hold them responsible for changes in American tastes, the more powerful they grow.

OK Marketing

by Duke of URL

IF AN expert marketing staff was all that was necessary to successfully bring a product to market, we'd all be eating McRibs, watching Chevy Chase, dressing Hasidic chic, and listening to Hootie and the Blowfish.

Some of the most memorable examples of products falling victim to the big bozo filter of the masses spurt forth from the soft drink industry. For our money, the swift counteroffensive to the "New Formula Coke" stratagem was at least as exhilarating a show of force as any Desert Storm shenanigans. And the only thing clearer than Crystal Pepsi was the fact that it would bomb.

Eighty percent of new products fail – as is appropriate, considering the general ineptitude governing their conception and marketing. But the fact that the public routinely exercises its discretion to be capricious shoppers is encouraging – in the master/slave game of consumerism, we consumers are the ones holding the whip, whether we like it or not.

And so, even though it seems to go against every vague principle we hold dear, we can't help feeling that **OK Soda,** the once-contentious icon of overobvious youth marketing, was an unfortunate victim of friendly fire. Maybe we just got trigger-happy once we saw through Subaru's shallow attempts to associate a car with "punk rock." In cases like that, the pitch not only fails to resonate, but actually reverse-resonates (detonates, perhaps?) – one imagines very disappointing quarterly reports.

From the Original OK Soda Homepage:
"Will Teens Buy It?," Time *magazine*
(May 30, 1994)
http://spleen.mit.edu/OK/article5.html
"Getting messages across to audiences
that don't fully realize they are receiving
them is as old as the subliminal spots for
popcorn and soda that advertisers flashed
on movie screens in the 1950s. What dis-
tinguishes Coke's campaign is that few of
the global companies pursuing teenagers
these days have been so elaborately slick in
inventing ways to be unslick." Time's early
analysis of OK could be more easily evisc-
erated for completely missing the point, if it
hadn't so presciently mirrored the public
reception. Arriving on the cusp of a flood of
overt, well-scrutinized "Gen X" marketing,
the dominant reaction to OK amongst its
target demographic was one of mistrust
and suspicion, as if the product were a
malignant swindle rather than a simple
instantiation of admirably obsequious pan-
dering. Then again, when the manufactur-
ers of "the real thing" attempt to corner the
market on the unreal thing as well, it's not
shocking that people would get bent out
of shape.

The tragedy of OK Soda, though, wasn't that it didn't resonate, but that it resonated too well.

Obviously, the debate has long since passed – even *alt.fan.ok-soda* has long been hijacked by wayward Usenetters looking for a quiet water-ing hole. But in the pages of magazines and design annuals, the sight of OK can designs, promotional items, and dispensing machines gets us weeping torrents into our tumblers.

The illustrators used, gleaned from the **Fantagraphics** stable, aren't exciting because they're great comix artists, but because they've masterfully bypassed the whole pathetic "art"-by-committee collabora-tive approach prevalent throughout major media. Through the con-temptible medium of comic books, they've found a low-key outlet for personal visual expression in pop culture (albeit marginal pop culture).

Generally, it's more amusing than annoying when Volkswagen fea-tures Psychic TV in its television commercials and "grunge" becomes the dominant leitmotif for Extreme Championship Wrestling. It's like Flint-stones Vitamins – no matter how much you dress them up, they're just vit-amins. But quite apart from its value as window dressing, OK Soda, like

any canned or bottled beverage, was bound to have some kind of graphic design (if only to distinguish it from Royal Crown). Why not decent art instead of that ubiquitous Dynamic Ribbon Device™?

Unfortunately, they blew it. By all reports, the drink's flavor had all the appeal of backwash, and even the kindest reviewer could do no better than "slightly spicy."

But, collectively, we blew it too. Think about it. In the brand-identity singles bar, it makes little sense to blow off the best-looking item around. It's one thing to be insulted by an inept come-on – the gold-chained Lothario whose spittle runs down your neck when he tries to whisper in your ear. It's another thing entirely to spurn the advances of a suitor whose impeccable style is marred by something as trivial as taste.

Perhaps our nostalgia comes from a source only a little deeper than the stack of design rags by our side. Perhaps we thirst for OK (or at least the cans) because when we steal a glance in the pop-culture rearview mirror, we see ourselves. In retrospect, OK's enthusiastic embrace of the marketing process was only slightly tighter than our own. From warning 1-800 callers that "your comments may be used in advertising or exploited in some other way we haven't figured out yet," to the obviously overoptimistic assumption that "the audience is in on the joke," OK's blatant hucksterism was shameless.

Fantagraphics

http://www.fantagraphics.com/
Independent filmmakers get their own cable channel. Independent musicians get heavy rotation on MTV. Independent comics artists languish in desolate obscurity. So much for the power of the pen. In the face of public indifference, Fantagraphics Books, led by the vocal and perennially indignant Gary Groth, has been publishing the best of the industry since 1976. Home of intransigently talented writer/artists such as Chris Ware, Al Columbia, and Dan Clowes, Fantagraphics books are often hard to find, but easy to spot – the creative roster favors artists dedicated to flawlessly capturing the errata of "a sad and beautiful world." Their works are as far from Batman comics as Ella Fitzgerald is from the Spice Girls. And with their website quickly evolving into a useful primer and catalog, their secret may finally find its way out, just where it belongs.

If we had been in the test-market areas, OK would be alive today. Bottles would stack up, untrashed, unrecycled. Our desks would be unreachable, landfills would fully decompose, and street people would be looking elsewhere for redeemable deposits, because we'd no sooner trash a six-pack than an *Eightball*.

So here's a thought: Why not send us your empty bottles, your promotional mobiles, your – dare we dream it – OK vending machines? To you, such items are the rubble left from a marketing bomb; to us, they have the cold beauty of shadows left etched on the pavement The Day After. In exchange for any OK propaganda we receive, we offer Suck paraphernalia – the only items whose future appears as murky as OK's past.

Mission: Implausible

by Polly Esther

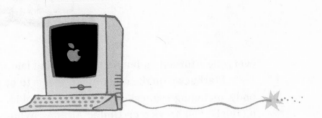

IN A country where carbonated beverages are romanticized more than marriage, far-fetched marketing schemes hardly register on the absurdity radar. But Apple's cross-promotional campaign with Paramount Pictures had all the subtlety of a radio wristwatch or a self-destructing tape player. Apple TV ads featured a *Mission: Impossible* theme, including clips from the movie and the slogan: "After you see the movie, why not pick up the Book?" The PowerBook, get it?

While arbitrarily linking a Hollywood movie and a floundering high-tech company might, indeed, seem like an impossible mission, the perceived ridiculousness of tie-in promotions fades as their pervasiveness increases. Suddenly it seems that almost any two products can become bedfellows, no matter how odd the couple.

Take Travelodge, a company which has reportedly experienced a 10 to 15 percent annual growth rate since using tie-in promotions, including one cross-promotion with Paramount Pictures' *Congo* and Citgo gasoline. BMW's tie-in with *Goldeneye* was perhaps a bit more appropriate – even though Bond usually drives an Aston Martin. Then there's Hewlett-Packard, cross-promoting with Disney Interactive, or McDonald's, cross-promoting with every Hollywood blockbuster for the family – though we still expect nicotine patches to start showing up in "Happy Hour Meals," now that the clown's all grown up.

Naturally, the web is a swirling sea of cross-promotions – they're just so easy to do. Link trading, listing search engines, listing news services, listing the coffee the webmaster drinks. . . . It's an orgy, where

everyone's turned on but no one's getting laid.

Starbucks, on the other hand, seems to be getting a piece of everybody, including real estate in Barnes & Noble, American Express commercials, and service on United Airlines. While it's hard to believe anyone cares that much about a hill of (coffee) beans, let's keep in mind that it's the brand, not the product, that matters, and the brand is all about eliciting positive associations. When you're squished into a tiny airplane seat, with a sluggy egg loaf perched ominously in front of you, that Starbucks' cup might just bring to mind a sunny afternoon on a shop-lined street, where you bought that fabulous blue silk Ann Taylor that you wore to Gigi's last cocktail party. . . . Suddenly the skies seem just a little friendlier. Or trendier, anyway.

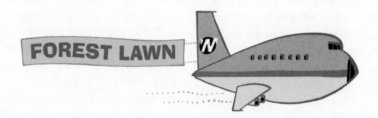

But the skies can't get much friendlier, as long as airlines are teaming up with just about anyone in their frequent flyer programs, offering deals on rental cars, credit cards, hotels, florists, long-distance phone services. Since every purchase leaves consumers feeling like they've accomplished something, like they're "saving" for a vacation, no less, the popularity of such programs isn't hard to grasp. "All I have to do is charge US$3,000 more on my American Advantage Miles Visa, and we're off to Club Med!" In the world of marketing promotions, that's a win-win situation equivalent to landing the Pope as your celebrity spokesperson.

Of course, celebrity endorsements are just another form of cross-promotion, as stars are essentially promoting themselves as products along with the product or service they represent. Once you recognize that such endorsements can help to improve celebs' careers by giving them visibility they might not find elsewhere, it's hard not to scrutinize stars' moves for hidden agendas – maybe Johnny Depp's "Winona Forever" tattoo wasn't true love at all, but a cross-promotional scheme dreamt up by their managers.

Tie-ins are consistently successful, and we can hope to see many, many more. Says Caryn Crump, Shell brand positioning manager, of a promotion with motor-sports sponsorships: "We want to start having a continuous Shell message in the marketplace, continuously offering promotions and events and reasons for consumers to keep coming back." So the reasons for coming back are not the product itself, but instead the promotions and events – sort of like going to the prom dateless, just for the petit fours. (A shudder of familiarity overcomes us. . . .)

When you consider all the possibilities, you realize that never before has it been easier to be a marketing executive – just spin the product wheel, and pick 2 to 4 from the following list: a model, an actress, a fictional character on a sitcom, a cartoon, a beverage, a fast food, a perfume, an airline, a retail clothing store, a Hollywood blockbuster, a video store, a "high-tech" or "cutting-edge" company. The cycle continues endlessly, with Internet service providers marketing with sodas and breakfast cereals, perfume tie-ins with romantic comedies, record companies cross-promoting with Cheez Whiz.

Soon it's impossible to tell the promoters from the promoted – choices begin to seem organic. What other soft drink would our friends on *Friends* drink but Diet Coke? They're hot, they're slender, they wear Levi's (isn't a girl wearing Levi's in one of those Classic Coke commer-

McDonald's: Official Restaurant of the NBA
http://www.mcdonalds.com/a_sports/ sportsnba
Of all the comarketing cocktails, those involving McDonald's and anything vaguely related to sports and/or physical fitness are amongst the most stomach-upsetting.

cials?), and when they're not drinking Diet Coke they're drinking milk. And getting it all over their upper lips, which is really pretty disgusting.

And if they drive cars, they're probably Miatas. And if they wear T-shirts with little pockets, they're probably from The Gap. And if they wear sneakers, they're probably Airwalks. And if they had an NBA star on the show, it would probably be Michael Jordan, except he'd be wearing a Hanes pocket T and Nikes. So there might be a fight, which would be on Pay-Per-View, unless that violates Jordan's contract, since NBC is covering the NBA. But before the fight, they'd have to play Paula Abdul, since she thinks Coke is It, and so do the Friends, except that Paula was once a Laker Girl. . . .

Given the endless conflicts these cross-promotions create, the formation of various competing consumer groups or parties seems inevitable, in which each demographic has a number of lifestyle packages to choose from: will you be a Pottery Barn/Victoria's Secret/Virgin Records/Heineken Frequent Buyer, or would you prefer to be a Crate & Barrel/Frederick's/Tower Records/Guinness Consumer Club Member?

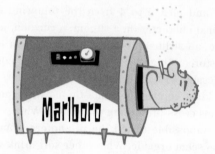

Fact is, there are so many other promotional opportunities as plain as the clogged pores on your Sara Lee-snarfing face. We imagine trading in forty lids from pints of Ben & Jerry's for one free week at Nautilus. Every fiftieth case of Bud could earn us one free month at the Betty Ford Clinic. And that two hundredth carton of Salem Lights? Perhaps it would be worth a coupon for US$200 off a plot at the local boneyard, for the rapidly approaching time when we're no longer "alive with pleasure."

NikeTown Crier

by St. Huck

HIGH above Bryant Street in San Francisco, there's an eye-catching billboard. More flag than ad, it features no text and no photographs – just a black background, a red oval, and that ubiquitous white swooshstika. Like the twentieth century's most notorious logo, from which it appropriates its color scheme and bold graphic style, the Nike billboard is a highly effective piece of iconography, galvanizing teenage thugs and suburban housewives alike with its symbolic magic. It announces the debut of Nike's retail presence in Union Square, but staring up at it, it's easy to imagine that the company's new chain of stores, extravagant as they are, are mere prelude to a far grander vision of corporate sovereignty.

Even wearing Air Jordans, it's a giant leap from NikeTown to NikeState, but Nike CEO Phillip Knight, like any multibillionaire, must entertain at least occasional dreams of the status that statesmanship might afford him. After all, isn't fashion just fascism with more emphasis on uniforms than ammunition? Every time a new NikeTown opens, the faithful come in droves to pledge their fealty to Knight's vision: eight-year-olds break their piggybanks to buy overpriced wristbands; aging Yuppies dress golf cap to walking shoe in the emperor's new clothes. The patriotic equivalent of consumer devotion is increasingly rare today; even the militia movement can't match the brandinistas for numbers. Wandering the retail mazes of the nation's NikeTowns, passively absorbing the totalitarian adspeak that adorns the walls, they wait for their call to arms, restless and dutiful.

SALES HEIL!

"Mall of the Wild," by Hans Eisenbeis
http://www.feedmag.com/96.12eisenbeis/
96.12eisenbeis.html

It may be hard to believe, but the Mall of America isn't just a metaphor; it's also an actual mall. But while Hans Eisenbeis, in "Mall of the Wild" on Feed, finds a profound sense of wrongness in the Minneapolis consumer cavern's Rainforest Cafe, auto dealerships, Knott's Camp Snoopy, and FAO Schwartz Barbie Store, one still shouldn't lose sight of the phenomenon's far-flung analogs. Take the Plaza de Las Americas in San Juan, Puerto Rico. Also the size of a medium-sized hamlet, Plaza de Las Americas has recently found a novel method of synergizing its medical office annex with its sprawling retail space: beepers. Rather than flipping through the latest issue of _iHola!_ in the waiting areas, patients are given beepers and invited to shop until they're called. For all the talk of the anxiety-producing effects of modern consumer capitalism, shopping still tends to be less stressful than oral surgery.

Isn't it time, finally, to fully implement the corpornation, the real Mall of America? As long ago as 1946, Peter Drucker was declaring the corporation America's representative social institution; in the fifty years since then, corporate influence upon our lives has become so routinely all-pervasive it's hard to remember it wasn't always that way. Until the late 1800s, though, corporations were chartered only for specific purposes and durations, with additional limits on land ownership and capitalization; now all it takes to start one is ten spare minutes and a few hundred bucks.

Today, the few people who dream of resurrecting those original restrictions are either dismissed as purveyors of parannoying cant or totally ignored. As for the rest of us, well, except for the most egregious displays of multinational malice, all is permitted. That's how it goes when you're in love – and really, which of the following institutions evoke the strongest feelings of ardor these days: Nike, Starbucks, and Nintendo, or Congress, the Executive Office, and the FBI? There's certainly no one building fan pages for Louis Freeh.

As much as we'd like to declare ourselves citizens of our favorite

MEDIA

$

CLINTON

brands, most corporations are probably somewhat less inclined to have us. Even if citizenship were invitation-only, corporation-states would still lose out on the hundreds of billions of dollars available to them now as corporate wealthfare. There'd be no more taxes, but also no more subsidies, bargain-basement land deals, or overseas co-op marketing campaigns. And without the divertissement of political scandal, public scrutiny of corporate behavior would likely intensify. There's a reason Clinton attracts more corporate support than any previous Democrat; his virtuoso facility for courting federal investigations makes him an excellent media baffle. With the press so engaged in deep-throating the details of botched blow jobs, there's less bandwidth to spend on corporate snow jobs.

On the other hand, given the current climate of consumer indifference to corporate iniquity, maybe baffles like Clinton aren't really necessary anymore. Outside NikeTown's San Francisco grand opening, activists protesting the company's employment practices in Indonesia were met with apathetic shrugs. What was it the ordinary Germans said in response to Hitler's diabolical directive: just do it? To assuage the few reporters who've shown more interest in sweatshops than shopping for sweats, Nike recently hired freelance Samaritan Andrew Young to put a positive spin on the situation – but in the land of NikeState, that kind of corporate rhinoplasty would be superfluous. Dissenters would be banished to the Birkenstock Nation.

Deliverance from government regulation and PC activism would certainly be enough to make some corporations embrace the new world order. Cigarette companies could forsake their strained attempts at stealth marketing and return to the good old days of honest, aggressive addiction cultivation. McDonald's could threaten rainforests with impunity, and cosmetics companies could start tarting up bunnies like drag queens again.

Of course, too much corporate self-interest would still have dire consequences; consider the case of the Republic of Cuervo Gold, a small

Ending Corporate Governance

http://www.ratical.com/corporations/
"It is essential to understand how corporations prior to the Civil War were legislatively defined, so we may better appreciate what we can discover and make use of today, using the sections still present in our state constitutions – as well as reinstating and strengthening in favor of nature, citizens, and communities many sections that have been repealed by corporate groups seeking to make incorporation laws more 'corporate-friendly' – to overthrow corporate authority, and reinstate the authority of we the sovereign people."
Sure, it bears an eerie resemblance to the creed of the People's Republic of Texas, but secessionist doctrine often follows well-worn tenets: appeals to the letter of the law, often of previous centuries; tightly delineated populist jingoism; and, always, an alternative rewrite of history, often not wholly unfounded. The authors of this digital broadside incite toward a revolt against the corporate plutocracy. While the plausibility of their liberated citizen's revolution may be on par with a flat-earther overthrow of NASA, they do provide a fascinating historical retrospective of the history of the corporation, reminding neophyte sovereigns that prior to the mid-1880s, corporations had limited durations, limited allowances on ownership of land, limited capitalization, limited purpose, and unlimited liability.

island country in the West Indies founded last year by the forward-thinking tequila makers. Despite its huge surplus of smarmy guy-life 'tude, the Republic is languishing – apparently no one can exist on (or stand) tequila, sand, and Cuervo Gold Ambassador **Dan Cortese** for more than a few hours. To succeed in a world of corporation-states, strategic alliances would be more necessary than ever.

How such partnerships all sort out, however, is ultimately incidental. The important thing about the evolution from nation-state to corpornation is how this change would reinvest our lives with meaning. With religion reduced to little more than vaporware and PR, and patriotism a mere marketing technique for celebrities who can't sing or act, we have few real opportunities to seriously express our belief in anything. We love our brands, yes, but what can you do to show that love except buy lots of crap and maybe make a Snapple commercial? A world of corporation-states would inevitably present more meaningful ways to prove faith: Whopper vs. Big Mac? Now that's a war worth fighting.

Milking It

by E. L. Skinner

Scampaign '96: The Charade Continues
*http://www.comedyusa.com/Scampaign/
Charade.new/GotTobaccoDrinkMilk.html*
Bob Dole, while reputed to possess an
adroit sense of humor, rarely succeeded in
making a fool of anyone but himself in the
'96 election. One memorable blunder
amongst many was his bungled attempt
to spin his way out of allegations of big
tobacco servitude by claiming that cigarettes may not be addictive. Hoping to add
some perspective, Dole added that some
probably think milk is dangerous to children. In the end, most people simply con-
cluded that Dole was more dangerous to
children than both putative vices combined.
In the interim, hack Leno-wannabe comics
mined such fertile comments for laffs, generally to no remarkable effect. For a sample, *comedyusa.com*'s archives provide
pages upon pages of Scampaign '96 commentary.

JUST when everything seemed to be winding down into a
pleasant premillennial apocalypse, with the world
degenerating into random violence, loveless sex, and another two years
of a Republican majority, along came the massive media blitz for a product almost synonymous with wholesomeness: milk.

Stealing what little thunder there was in the general election, the
National Fluid Milk Producers Promotion Board brashly Photoshopped
milk mustaches onto stock photos of Bill and Bob, without seeking or
receiving permission. When media observers, pundits, and even the Prez
quietly expressed their concern, the milkmen of Madison Avenue
responded by asserting that the candidates were "public figures," and
therefore fair game. That'll be news to Nike executives, who've been
hoodwinked for years into paying "public figure" Michael Jordan millions of dollars to hawk their tennies.

But really, what other trade group could possibly have gotten away
with this stunt? What's Bob Dole gonna say, that he doesn't condone the
consumption of milk? (Well . . .) Is Bill Clinton seriously going to litigate
against Skim, 2-Percent, and Whole? Sadly, Malt-O-Meal and Tang may be
eager to follow suit and airbrush a bowl of mush or a glass of electric
Kool-Aid in front of a beaming Newt Gingrich, but in their heart of hearts
– which is to say, in their legal departments, often confused with other
prominent parts of the corporate body – they know they could never get
away with it. Besides, milk isn't a brand. It's practically a Kantian category. Look at it this way: Who or what do the good dairy producers of

America consider their competition? Beer? Odwalla?

True, it's been said with bluer words in seedier places, but we can't help ourselves: those milk mustaches don't look exactly, um, kosher. The vaguely obscene connotations of whatever that is on Tyra Banks' upper lip are all the more provocative for the absence of an actual glass of milk. And it's stimulating to consider how many celebs have suckled at the teat – from Spike Lee to Kristi Yamaguchi, Bob Costas to The Phantom (though we note that Ron Jeremy and Marilyn Chambers have apparently not yet been approached). Indeed, the unofficial organ of all pop culture in print, *Rolling Stone*, recently bowed to the cause, launching a major sweepstakes cosponsored with the milk people in which they invite readers to "create and design your own milk mustache ad." The *Stone* isn't so much going downhill as simply going down.

An unsentimental look at the role of milk in American culture might convince an unstable mind there's some unsavory conspiracy afoot. Recently there's been a lot of tut-tutting about product placements in public school curricula, but milk has been arriving at 10:10 A.M. in grades one through six for most of this century. You want more proof of a milk conspiracy? How about the whole racket of publishing photos of missing and abducted people on milk cartons – often using sophisticated computer programs to simulate the effects of aging? To suppose that the milk industry is involved in some ghastly form of white slavery which they both subsidize and rail against probably gives the quasi-governmental institute too much credit, but still. . . . What were those sleep-inducing blue mats in kindergarten really about, anyway? And what about the milk industry's mocking, throw-down-the-gauntlet URL, *www.whymilk.com*? Step aside, Trilateral Commission, Committee of 100, International Order of Oddfellows, and the Shining Path – here's the Milky Way.

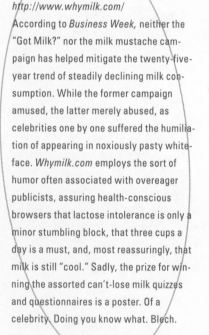

Milk – It's on Everybody's Lips
http://www.whymilk.com/
According to *Business Week,* neither the "Got Milk?" nor the milk mustache campaign has helped mitigate the twenty-five-year trend of steadily declining milk consumption. While the former campaign amused, the latter merely abused, as celebrities one by one suffered the humiliation of appearing in noxiously pasty white-face. *Whymilk.com* employs the sort of humor often associated with overeager publicists, assuring health-conscious browsers that lactose intolerance is only a minor stumbling block, that three cups a day is a must, and, most reassuringly, that milk is still "cool." Sadly, the prize for winning the assorted can't-lose milk quizzes and questionnaires is a poster. Of a celebrity. Doing you know what. Blech.

HAVE YOU SEEN ME?

On the other hand, there are some interesting political aspects of milk that haven't been fully exploited. For example, every snot-nosed kid knows that milk defines our whole phylum on the tree of life, mammals. Indeed, the word is cognate with *mammary* and *mama*. But the real issue at hand is why we exploit another species for our own daily dose of bone-building, teeth-whitening, libido-stoking milk. Here may be the solution to all our social ills; if Clinton were truly the bipartisan milkman of human kindness, he'd leverage his mandate to put welfare moms off the dole and on the milking machine. The national appetite for dairy could easily employ millions of freeloading women, killing two sacred cows with one stone.

From the look of it, the dairy industry wants you to believe their milk-mustache campaign is a public service announcement. Any company worth its dividends would trade its milk teeth for that kind of consumer confusion. But in light of recent reports about the chemical abuse of dairy cattle, the extinction of the family farm, price fixing, and the real possibility that drinking milk may be no more healthful than not drinking milk, it's clear that Land O' Lakes, Kemps, Old Home, and all the others are hedging their bets against a possible outbreak of that dread disease, lactose intolerance. And with the status they enjoy as America's favorite uncarbonated beverage that isn't bourbon, who can blame them for doing what comes naturally, and milking their market share for all it's worth?

All the World's a Stage

by Ann O'Tate

"The Virtualization of Electronic Public Space," by Tracie L. Streltzer
http://www.fau.edu/divdept/commcatn/pubspace.htm
A little-known aspect of Marshall McLuhan's infectious aphorisms on the emerging "Global Village" is that the global networks of today differ substantially from his perceived future. "McLuhan conceived of a passive audience of consumers, as opposed to an active public, participating freely and concurrently," writes Streltzer in the redundantly titled *The Virtualization of Electronic Public Space*. While it's easy to overestimate the actual significance of spontaneous group interaction amongst strangers (unless you're an entrepreneur in the adult industry), a fundamental lesson of digital media is that, love it or loathe it, it's still pretty much all our fault. Unlike Pauly Shore movies, for instance.

WHEN Marshall McLuhan described the future as a global village, he didn't mention that it would be a Planet Hollywood. Our dance around the electronic campfire was to be orchestrated by information architects, not entertainment engineers, and we were supposed to be sharing knowledge, not Cap'n Crunch-coated chicken tenders (only $6.95).

True, fiber-optic cable is folding together the four corners of the earth, yet this peculiar psychic origami has yet to change the shape of Americans' interactions with the rest of the world. Uncomfortable in any country where we can't get lite beer, quality toilet paper, and/or a souvenir T-shirt, we're still tourists, not neighbors, on most parts of the planet.

That's the comfort of Planet Hollywood, a menu-driven microcosm that replicates an increasingly homogeneous international box office. With most of the top-grossing films in the world made in America, Planet Hollywood's staggering solipsism is perhaps less narcissistic than prophetic. It was exactly this promise of global domination on a homunculoid scale, one mediocre restaurant at a time, that investors were counting on in April 1996 when they bid up the price of Planet Hollywood's initial public offering from US$18 to US$27 per share.

But these monuments to abstraction, it turns out, share a common fate with the more obvious descendants of McLuhan's line. Like net.stocks, the value of both Planet Hollywood's "actual props" and its shares relies as much (or more) on faith and novelty as on glamour or

scarcity. (Well, at least the stock's still worth the paper it's printed on.) At first glance, news of the restaurant chain's financial straits seems like the punch line to some Anthony Robbins parable, an apocryphal fable of a business too successful to succeed. But in the case of Planet Hollywood, the story isn't so much about Midas' touch as Morpheus': even spectacles can put people to sleep. And so last quarter's reports revealed what any Adorno acolyte could have predicted, that profitability hinged upon an illusion of constant growth; the revenue stream of each individual restaurant, after a typically superheated opening, becomes as cold and sludgy as day-old Cajun Eggrolls.

The prospect of **Planet Hollywood's infinite expansion** – not an ideal business plan, but surely the most compelling – raises the question of whether illusions are, in fact, a renewable resource. Will there be enough fantasy to go around? A pessimist might predict a future where bitterly prosaic artifacts pose as props. Sadly, you can't satirize such a vision – it's a joke that relies too heavily on ignoring the small space in San Francisco's Planet Hollywood devoted to James Caan's mukluks

GENUINE RELIC MANUFACTURING COMPANY

"The Fetish of the New: Culture and Class in Alasdair Gray's Something Leather," by Stephen Baker

http://www.arts.gla.ac.uk/www/english/ comet/others/glasgrev/baker.html

Though not quite wielding the significance of Chomsky or Derrida as a cultural Prada bag, Theodor Adorno wrote extensively and promiscuously enough that his work can be hijacked as a vehicle to explain everything from the dislocating aspects of cyberspace to the meaningful congruences of shopping and S&M (which is how it is used here). Those in pursuit of understanding – and not a degree – are encouraged to seek out one of his less-cited works, *Minima Moralia,* a collection of brief observations written during Adorno's exile in Los Angeles from Nazi Germany. While never completely escaping the careful blandness that haunts most academic prose, the tenor of Adorno's vitriol towards capitalism in general and Los Angeles in particular makes the book at least as engaging an indictment of American popular culture as any Rage Against the Machine album.

People *Magazine Presents – The Planet Hollywood Locations*

http://pathfinder.com/people/planetholly wood/world.html

The battle to brand the globe is no sport for the meek (just ask Reebok). Never mind conscripting the patriots; think of the logistics. Apparently, Planet Hollywood's worldwide HQ map was too unwieldy to reliably codify without a strategic military alliance. Who better than *People*? People who need *People* are the luckiest people, they say, but we think they may simply have realized that you can't rule the world without 'em.

(from *Misery!*) and Tim Curry's Girl Scout uniform (from, er, *Loaded Weapon?*)

Much of the credit for Planet Hollywood's success has been given to architect David Rockwell (it remains to be seen if he'll be blamed for its failings); his participatory panoramas and three-dimensional Hockney paintings are so perfect in their representation of mass entertainment that they tend to drive cultural critics to either hyperbolic praise or apoplectic silence. For the smartass semiotician, Planet Hollywood presents just another a sad stereovision of the world, familiar to anyone who has read enough Debord or even just watched a lot of *USA Up All Night*.

Rockwell's ability to make celluloid dreams plastic reality has made him a sought-after builder on America's boulevard of broken themes. He's been called upon to design for all of Hollywood's biggest power brokers – from Warner Brothers to Sony to Robert De Niro. Rockwell's Mohegan Sun Casino cobbled together a mythology for a tribe whose identity is more literary than literal, turning Lady Luck into Pocahontas but still preferring cold hard cash to wampum. His real gamble, however, would be to call the bluff of the interviewer who last year asked what kind of pedestal Rockwell would carve for America's other blind goddess. "I'd make a diorama of it," he replied, "I'd have enormous pictures of lawyers like F. Lee Bailey."

Well, of course. Recreation obviously requires a certain degree of redundancy. The producers of O. J.-by-the-sea have tried hard to provide the same drama as Act I, but they've suffered the same mixed blessings that plague all sequels: the conventions have been conveniently established, yet the talent just isn't quite as fresh. In their daily reenactments, the faux jurists on E! sound like the idealized aliens of '50s sci-fi, showing a distinct discomfort with contractions, and a hesitating cadence that might cover either groping for a word or telepathic communication. And while there's no discernible reason for the sub-security-cam cinematography but continuity, the occasional stilted off-camera intonements bring to the proceedings a Greek chorus of unintended sobriety.

If the O. J. reenactments were just bad television – which they are – the appearance of Daryl Gates on the expert panel would be laughable instead of the next logical step in his burgeoning entertainment career. Likewise, the head-spinning metastasis of E!'s dramatizations of the civil trial's own reenactments would inspire knowing chuckles instead of news-addled nausea. As it is, the cable courtroom antics are only a concession stand away from an IPO, and it seems more than likely that Planet Hollywood will soon be filling the prop gap with a pair of bloody gloves.

The Writing's on the Stall

by Duke of URL

THE renowned deviant humorist Sigmund Freud once proposed anal birth as a universal theory amongst children, particularly boys. Carl Jung, striking a similarly profound victory on behalf of downtrodden crackpots everywhere, improved the notion, observing the excremental mortar binding diverse creation myths of both mankind and the Earth itself. Predictably, though, it took the marketing visionaries at Addison Wesley Longman and Bantam Books to put a hundred years worth of shitpot wisdom in its place: namely, the hands of toilet-obsessed preteens.

A million defaced bumpers testify to the fact that shit happens, but until recently, this insight has been lost on everyone but Mr. Whipple. Sure, breathtaking scatological panoramas didn't hurt *Trainspotting*, but soiling the minds of the most naturally receptive consumers – the kids – is a trickier proposition. The deft rim shots of the past, ranging from the Garbage Pail Kids all the way back to the classic Toilet Talker, often failed to slide by parental filters. Convincing parents to pitch in for what amounts to a commodified catalyst for deep-seated shame and humiliation clearly demanded strategy. In fact, it demanded science.

With the sundry excretory and eliminative bodily functions gathered under the proprietary rubric of Grossology™, biology instructor Sylvia Branzei launched not only a successful line of books, but also a booming cottage industry. Recognizing the visceral fizzle of fried worms compared to gonzo gastroenterology, publishers responded with *Gross Anatomy*, *The Gas We Pass*, *Everyone Poops*, *Gross Grub*, and the

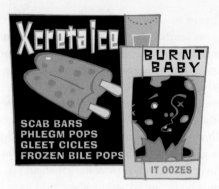

Xcreta Ice

BURNT BABY

SCAB BARS
PHLEGM POPS
GLEET CICLES
FROZEN BILE POPS

IT OOZES

groundbreaking *Barf-O-Rama*™ series. The sales were nothing short of gastroincredible, and Branzei's grossology brand is in development as a TV series, no doubt pitched as *School-Outhouse Rock*.

The point isn't science, really, even though correct pronunciation of *coprophagy* (caw-PRUF-fa-jee) amongst youngsters is far from trivial. A media climate where one can't even watch good old-fashioned trash TV without an ugly TV-M bug marring the screen demands increased overt rationalization. Bullshit legitimizing logic acts as a knowing wink between the producer and the consumer, and while both are wont to be caught up in their own rhetoric, it's mainly for the sake of prudes and parents that such overtures are sung. And this ruse has come a long way since the "ethnographic films" of bare-assed natives and nudist camps of yesteryear.

Barf-O-Rama
http://www.bdd.com/barforama
The little ones simply must read, for reading brings knowledge and knowledge is power. The Barf-O-Rama line of juvenile-oriented literature may mislead — it's actually a quite edifying body of work, hipping kids to highbrow culture under the guise of fecal high jinks. How else to explain loaded terms such as "Beethoven movements" (noun. From the popular dog movies, meaning dog doo.)? This and other vocabulary builders, such as "Benji movements," are conveniently available at the Barf-O-Rama Icktionary online resource.

POOPY'S
SCRATCH
&
SNIFF
FUN
BOOK

POOPY

Animal Grossology, *by Sylvia Branzei*
Coprophagy: "The scientific name for caca-eating is coprophagy (caw-PRUF-fa-jee). This word comes from the Greek words kopr-, or dung, and -phagos, or eating. Seems like dookie munching has been around a long time."

Today's information entrepreneurs are probably wondering how far it can be pushed. Nobody watches *Real Stories of the Highway Patrol* to study departmental policy – we're just hoping to see the transcendent moment where a cop's billy club meets a perp's head. What is the current lineup of weekend TV pathology if not "crime does not pay" moved from the pages of a comic book and redrawn on the little screen, with an emphasis on scarlet? If there exists the slightest possibility that it'll get little Johnny to read or even think, prospects abound. Perhaps an intro to chemistry could be spiced up by demonstrating the effects of industrial-strength cleaning products on Rover's larynx?

Alarmists might shake their heads, but educators have reason to see this trend as the biggest breakthrough since art teachers alerted kids to the logic of Elmer including a picture of a bull on his glue. Nobody wants to hear the good news; that's what the ads are for. A blob of fake birdshit on the cover of *Animal Grossology* instead propels the content toward its apogee, a delicious ad and product unto itself. And if it can be marketed as edifying – well, let's just say *The People vs. Larry Flynt* was up for five Golden Globes.

The real fear is that flatulent preadolescents, having had their outlets for shock value indulged, will kill the market by getting over it. But though the first ten years of our lives might see us inhabiting ten separate demographics, neoconsumers are born every minute, each with an adorably short memory. Take *BabyMugs,* an infant-oriented videocassette that simply shows the faces of other babies, and has proven a smash sensation among toddlers. Give them a few years and they'll be whacking the shit out of chainsaw-wielding goblins on their Nintendo 64s, but by then, a new generation will already have been ushered in.

And the "beauty part," as the VPs might say, is that come age sixteen, the same kids will be driving their beat-up Miata junkers to Urban Outfitters, where the Barf-O-Rama line of literature, now safely coated in the patina of retro, already resides. Of course, allowing for the spiral of the kitsch quotient, by then they'll probably be back to reading Freud.

HYPER VEXED

The more we get into technology, the more it gets into us. New media, new tools, new careers – to the extent that we accept them, metaphors for living are forced upon us, sometimes welcome, sometimes smothering. Often, they simply go unnoticed.

How long did it take for people to notice that the remote control, as a handheld locus of "free will," was a more profound invention than the television itself? That the MPAA ratings attached to movies often say as much about societal boundaries as the films themselves? That interstate highways and speeding tickets would come to represent not just the extent of our dependence on cars, but perhaps the most tangible argument in favor of federal government most of us are willing to appreciate?

McLuhan paved the way for such technometaphor-spelunking when he rechristened almost every human invention "media," and tagged them all as "extensions of man." It was a welcome concept, at the very least it was preferable to equating technology with icecubes and searching for hidden sex, but the utility of his theory has clearly reached its half-life. Today's tech breakthroughs are as much about constricting as extending, often supplanting the more banal functions of the human machine altogether.

When one thinks of the impact of computers and information networks, it's often easy to concentrate on speed – the speed at which a machine can crunch numbers and data and the Internet can relay bits and bytes. But what of memory? What happens when our every correspondence, both written and spoken, can be effortlessly archived in perpetuity? Will we choose to haunt our grandchildren with time-released capsules of digital posterity, vividly reminding them that their long-deceased elders were every bit as naïve and inarticulate as their flat-screen electronic encyclopedias led them to believe? We may want to eulogize our passings now in preparation for that day when we're deleted for the second, and final, time.

Looking to the world of videogames, which adherents are quick to point out is bigger business than both movies and music, we're faced with yet another ploy to mend, fluff, and Martinize the fabric of reality in the emergence of virtual first-person 3-D spaces.

Not the kind you chat in (those are going bankrupt faster than you can name them), but the kind you kill in. Browsing through gaming magazines, it's easy to find ads for services such as Heat.net, a multiplayer game network, with copy cheekily promising to "create a peaceful reality through violent cyberspace!" "War is not a rational decision; it's instinctive," the ad proclaims. "The answer is not to stop killing; the answer is to change the way we kill – by taking it to the net . . . HEAT IS THE ANSWER!" The ad's a farce, but possibly not completely untrue, if a larger trend toward separation of entertainment and reality holds its course. But if we interact with others in the same unreal places where killing at will (or flaming, at least) isn't a crime, does that reduce the social arena to mere entertainment? Or merely remind us that it always was?

Sifting, accepting, or rejecting the deluge of would-be

transforming tools is as much a function of age as it is of ideology. Those with perspective might tend toward conservatism, fearful of a New World Order shepherded by Super Mario and Duke Nukem; the rest of us will be content to avoid novel paradigms with per-minute charges. As long as the software and hardware sold to us help us kill time without murdering our bottom lines, we'll let it live. And if it forces us to reevaluate our concepts of self and society, we'll try not to hold that against it.

"Thinking Outside the Mailbox" is Polly Esther's taxonomy of email prevarication, a useful primer on the modern methods of saying one thing while meaning another thing entirely or, sometimes, nothing at all. Neophyte Internet correspondents would do well to temper her exhortations toward Eudoraphoria with the knowledge that she secretly deletes almost everything in her inbox. E. L. Skinner's "To Err is Human, To Crash Divine" is less a study of technology biting back than simply shutting down. Comparing the crashes of ValuJet with those of Netscape, Skinner notices a double standard at play, and finds justification for it via good old-fashioned theology.

Two opposing viewpoints toward work in the paperless office are presented in "Dining With Cannibals" and "Sub-Middle Management Worksick Blues," both presented anonymously for obvious reasons. "Dining With Cannibals" is an ur-geeksploitation rant, a trenchant fuck-you to the Silicon Valley CEO on behalf of every engineer who's ever worked an eighty-hour week for a handful of stock options. "Sub-Middle Management Worksick Blues," on the other hand, is a stress headache rendered in prose, a manager's frustrated sob upon seeing the best minds of a corporation driven to distraction by the very medium they set out to conquer.

Finally, Justine's inspired "Nite Crawler" is a memoir of the shame and discovery ignominiously sustained by a lonely night with a search engine. Justine details her ill-considered queries on lovers long forgotten and not forgotten enough, and how the answers she found were simultaneously shocking, misleading, and consummately revealing. In the future, we're forced to believe, everyone will be a stalker for fifteen minutes. And be stalked, we hasten to add, for a lifetime.

Thinking Outside the Mailbox

by Polly Esther

WHILE the odds of our reproducing anytime soon are generally better if the two Xs involved are at the fore and aft of *Xerox*, lately we've been thinking "The Days Before Email" would make an exciting story for our grandchildren. We'll be decrepit and incontinent and much, much more bitter, but doubtlessly as eager to bore our demon spawn as we are to bore you right now. We'll sit those little whippersnappers down and show them our Eudora registration card and speak of the days before Pine was felled. Incredulous, they'll squeak, "You were alive back then?!!" And we'll say, "Why sure! My God, was it a pain in the ass!" But they'll just squint quizzically at us for a second, and then run off to score some McCrack down the block. "Kids today!" we'll croak, and then forget the whole conversation.

As Michael Kinsley has shown, first-timers find that email rivals the curly-fry maker for social significance. And, as much as we like curly fries, they've done nothing to help us evade countless awkward or trying social situations on a daily basis. For that, we look to Eudora, and with her wisdom, guidance, and filters, we breeze through a world of Treach-erously Significant Social Interactions like Barry Sanders on speed.

If you can't recognize these various branches of the email taxon-omy, you'd better start flexing your digital muscles a little more. You've got social land mines to evade! As Faulkner once said, "I believe that man will not merely endure; he will email."

The Playing Hooky Email: One of our favorites. Perhaps you've got "an appointment." Perhaps you're "working" at home. Or maybe you're

"sick" or have "jury duty." Perhaps you're "hung over" or "depressed" or "having family problems" or "lazy." Maybe you're "shopping" or "skiing" or "lying on a beach drinking margaritas," or even "plotting to overthrow the government." Regardless, the Playing Hooky Email makes work avoidance easier than ever. Hammer out some lame excuse, press "send," and you're home free, all without a thought to your boss overhearing those rabble-rousing revolutionaries shouting and testing plastic explosives in the background. It's soooo easy, it makes you feel all dirty inside . . . only for a second, right before your third margarita.

The After-Work Plans Email: This email features comments regarding postwork social gatherings, including times, meeting places, pros and cons of each time and meeting place, each person's particular nutritional and emotional needs, scheduling requirements, etc. Typical messages contain such provocative prose as: "That okay?" or "Maybe. Where?" or "Probably. What time?" Individuals on the cc: list will also chime in with their own particular tastes, time restrictions, and personal hang-ups. The information exchanged boils down to a two-minute phone call, but takes about double the time of the social gathering being planned. In fact, studies indicate that After-Work Plans Emails cost the country billions upon billions of dollars in wasted labor, and the total time expended on such email interchanges nationwide is equal to the time it took to plan and build the Great Wall of China. But, conveniently, we don't need a wall, we need a beer, and the loss of billions of dollars

only makes the After-Work Plans Email a more effective revolutionary act than all those bomb-building sessions you've been wasting your sick days on.

The Long-Lost Friend Email: Every holiday season it happens again: Long-forgotten friends and acquaintances and friends of acquaintances begin shooting off "Hey, stranger!" emails like so many high school yearbook snapshots coming to life and jeering in your face. Suddenly, all your favorite revenge fantasies are foiled – gone is the vision of you, sweaty but glamorous, screaming into the mike: "This song, entitled 'You Bitch,' is dedicated to Kelly Atkins, who, in high school, did me the favor of stealing away the only man I ever loved. . . ." Instead, it's "Kelly Atkins <katkins@msn.com> Subject: Hi!" and in a split second, seething gyrations are replaced with a ten-minute summary of the last ten years. But you give it your best shot, reeling off lists of spectacular accomplishments and fabulous friends, replete with self-deprecating asides, all of which are totally transparent and pathetic, particularly to a manipulative slut like Kelly. But still, the Long-Lost Friend Email provides a rare chance at a casual boast, a veiled jab, or an insulting aside, and that makes it utterly irresistible to petty jerks like ourselves. We know you're just as bad.

The Ongoing Flirtation Email: You see him at a party. You know where he works. You like his shoes, and you need to tell him so. You slam off a quick email, edit it a few times so it's light, funny, nonchalant. He emails back. Such a sparkling wit! You reply: one-up a few insults, pay him a backhanded compliment, and include a humorous, somewhat zany digression that reflects your devil-may-care attitude (and hints at your extensive knowledge of Martin Amis). He swoons. Soon, you're checking your email every five minutes, and your heart races every time his name comes up. Your productivity suffers, but your job satisfaction skyrockets (not to mention your mastery of coy, witty prose). Finally, you meet him

for a beer. He's chafingly smug and seems practically pre-verbal in person. But you have to admit, those Ongoing Flirtation Emails made life much more interesting, if only for a little while. . . .

The Virtual Boss Email: Your boss doesn't like meeting with you, talking to you, or seeing your face, for that matter. So he sends off the occasional oblique remark, like "Ever come into the office these days?" or "What were you trying to get from this project?" – all in a tone so remote from the daily workings of the place as to seem otherworldly. He also regularly uses email to inform the staff of sweeping changes as if they're incidental, and attempts to throw in a democratic feel with exhortations to chime in your vote:

```
I was thinking that maybe it's time to abandon this
initiative you've spent months on and start from
scratch. Just 'cause "new" seems "better" somehow.
I might add that anyone who supports the "old" approach
is standing in the way of progress (and soon may be
standing in the unemployment line). All in favor?
```

Such "emails from the edge" can be utterly disconcerting, but if he delivered such messages face-to-face, your first reaction would be to serve up a piping-hot knuckle sandwich. Instead, you smoke a pack of filterless cigarettes, then concoct an unreasonably reasonable message like: "Thanks for the feedback!" or "What a great idea!" Thusly, the

Virtual Boss Email saves you your job and saves your boss a world of pain.

The Invisible Acquaintance Email: Everyone has them – an acquaintance they'd just as soon never see again. Maybe it's the way he slurps his beers. Maybe it's the way she talks endlessly about nothing and starts most sentences with the phrase "I'm the kind of person who. . . ." Whether it's guilt or a sense of shared history that compels you to maintain contact with them, or just dumb curiosity about how their lives are shaping up, you're destined to suffer the consequences: volleying back and forth inane little updates, all curiously devoid of concrete face-to-face plans, despite the fact that you live blocks away from each other. A chickenshit approach, indeed. Yet when you consider the alternative – sitting in a bar for hours, repeating the phrase "Sooo . . . how are . . . things?" – you recognize the immense value-add of the Invisible Acquaintance Email. It frees your life of hopelessly flaccid interactions – aside from the occasional cocktail party – once and for all.

The Ex Email: She dumped you two years ago, the fucking piece of shit. Because the parting was bitter, you haven't spoken to her since, except for the time you saw her at that bar when you were really drunk and you cried and told her you'd always love her. You don't love that bitch anymore, though, and you want her to know it. In fact, you're happier than you've ever been, and by all accounts your life is a whole hell of a lot better than hers. You won't rest until her last image of you as a total loser is replaced with your current glorious reality! In other words, you're still something of a loser, and you should probably just find a therapist, but instead you find her email address. She never emails you back, of course. There is no closure for losers, but at least now you can say you tried.

The Networking Email: Remember the first time someone introduced you to the concept of "networking"? Remember how you decided, right then and there, that you'd never have a decent job if it required calling your mother's friend from L.A. who sells medical supplies, pretending to have some interest in his "field"? Well, email has made networking as simple as Mrs. Smith's peach pie. So forget those painful, fumbled conversations in which your lack of attention to detail and total apathy toward work in general become painfully obvious. Just mix together a polite inquiry, a little obsequious fawning, a few proud statements regarding your superior attention to detail as evidenced by every second of your life, and then drop a few important names, preferably of blood relatives. Voilà! That frustratingly mundane, totally thankless job is yours!

The fact that email can make social interactions efficient, preformatted, and carefully controlled only comprises half of our Eudoraphoria. Email also provides a record of every single thing you've ever said or heard. Aspiring novelists and diarists need not carry around clumsy notebooks or little tape recorders disguised as packs of Marlboros – the full text of their lives is one "Save As" away. Those who've wondered where the year has gone, wonder no more. Every plan, every fight, every flirtation, every thwarted relationship, all of it lies in the bowels of your mailboxes just waiting to be archived forever and ever.

Indeed, simply by perusing the last few weeks of personal email, we're struck with an undeniable sense of longing and melancholy, thinking of all those poignantly innocent emails from our early digital days, trashed so carelessly, lost to youthful ignorance and the foolishness of the email neophyte.

We'll teach our grandchildren to avoid this mistake, if those little bastards would ever visit.

To Err Is Human,
To Crash Divine

by E. L. Skinner

WHEN *Animals Attack* isn't the only sick indulgence to carry on the tradition of decadence we once enjoyed in *Faces of Death*. Jonathan Harr's article in the *New Yorker* immersed its highbrow readership in an exquisitely gruesome flight disaster. The fact that it was a story without a conclusion is irrelevant: the surgical detail Harr relates in his telling of the 1994 crash and subsequent investigation of USAir Flight 427 is a sinful temptation to factory-installed human nature, which can neither look nor not look. Not since the "Woman" issue have Ms. Brown and company shown themselves to be quite so opportunistic; when planes started falling from the sky again this summer, they could finally go to press with this pulp nonfiction.

The crashes of TWA 800 and ValuJet 592 put a fine point on the bizarre compulsion we have to get to the bottom of flight disasters. Flying is an unnatural way for our species to travel. More to the point, it's an exceptionally horrific way to die. Thus, though we tolerate error, inaccuracy, and sloppy paperwork in almost all other aspects of modern life, there's simply got to be one helluva good reason for a plane to plant itself this way. If not (as the insurance industry so optimistically says) an Act of Nature, then it had better be the handiwork of a terrorist. Plain old mechanical failure is not an option, never has been. Sure, misguided faith is what lubes the wheels of most industries, but think about it – just how long was the advent of commercial air travel delayed by the discovery that Icarus plummeted due to human error?

Of course, digital crashes tend to be somewhat less threatening than analog ones, especially if you factor out the stock market, which is a kind of weird bridge between the two. In computing, regular folks have a high tolerance for error.

Consider, for example, Netscape's continual release of yet another Navigator in beta. Not only will we be up to our ears in Type 11s, we'll be happy about it, what with Netscape's "bug bounty" program in which churlish geeks worldwide will do the company's dirty work for the price of a lousy T-shirt. Now imagine the National Transportation Safety Board giving away those cool blue federal windbreakers to any passerby who happens to find a sticky valve or a blasting cap among the smoking debris of a crash site. Or imagine how many people would line up for the Boeing 747.03a in beta. Now that would put some teeth in the term *download*.

If only real-world crashes were more virtual, there'd be a lot less

Umberto Eco's Analogy – Mac:DOS as Catholic:Protestant
http://www.umds.ac.uk/elsewhere/cauty/eco.html
The clean logic of Eco's famous theological Mac:DOS syllogism is undermined only slightly by the current perception on Wall Street that the Pope resides in Redmond. With the Mac currently withering in the face of widespread apostasy, and DOS cast aside for more credible translations, though, one can't help but hope for an updated release of a new application of Eco techno-ecclesiastics. Would Eco see the Internet as Calvinistic, "demanding personal decisions, imposing a subtle hermeneutics upon the user, and taking for granted the idea that not all can reach salvation," while observing AOL to be Protestant, "cheerful, friendly, conciliatory, telling the faithful how they must proceed step-by-step to reach – if not the Kingdom of Heaven – the moment in which they've got mail?" Not until AOL becomes EOL, we're afraid.

cleaning up to do. More often than not, network crashes are actually freeze-ups. Try rolling that ergonomic office chair of yours over that gray Ethernet cord a few times – just as if you'd stepped on a garden hose, the packets will build up enormous pressure, which, when released, will easily flood your PC's IP stack. Your LAN will have the responsiveness – and approximate value – of a freezer-burned pork chop, and neither the patience of Job (nor Miracle Thaw) will thaw it out. Still, you've got what's left of your health, and there's always CTRL-ALT-DEL.

Unless you're a dyed-in-the-wool, card-carrying, pointy-headed code cruncher, it's hard to believe there's a rational reason for each error, glitch, and whatsit that announces itself on a typical workday. In reality, we prefer to believe there's a theological reason for every little unexplained fart that slips out of our Power Macs. Umberto Eco may have been the most famous pundit to identify the true War of the Roses going on between the platforms. But no matter what your denomination,

I/O errors seem to come around with roughly the same fleeting unpredictability as the Virgin Mary, Elvis, and any other paranormal phenomenon. As far as we're concerned, we just want the angels to beat the devils in the more influential precincts of our humble motherboards.

Ironically, analog technologies are far more forgiving. Like anything run through a dogma mill, the digital (and digerati's) reduction of everything to its binary signage tends to do real violence to the fuzzy products of human wetware. Computers and their papal inflexibility translate code with a logical precision that would shame a Salem Puritan. Hence the classic spellchecker fuckups that are apparent throughout even the most prestigious major media websites. They may not be crashing our system, but they're not doing much for our patience.

We know we should be more forgiving, but somehow we're as driven as the NTSB to get to the root of all error and weed it out. We want to do our part to keep the skies safe for browsers everywhere. At least we'd like to see a few more copy editors getting their seating assignments. All things considered, the web is still the safest way to die. Er, fly. Just make sure your hard drive is in a state of grace before you install the latest version of Navigator and walk up the gangway.

National Transportation Safety Board – Accident Synopses
http://www.ntsb.gov/Aviation/months.htm
Just as TWA should never consider screening *ConAir* for its passengers, one would be well advised to avoid using the seat-back modem link to browse the NTSB Accident Synopses aviation incident matrix. Stretching back almost fifteen years and conveniently disassembled into 170-plus jam-packed monthly charts of screwups big and small, the site conclusively disproves the notion that the skies you fly are friendly. In fact, they blow, sometimes literally. May we recommend *amtrak.com*, instead?

Dining with Cannibals

by POP

"Rage," by Mark Nollinger, Wired 2.06
http://www.hotwired.com/wired/2.06/
features/rage.html
It kills us to so recklessly plug our corporate patrons, but we've always kept *Wired*'s 1994 autopsy of systems-analyst-turned-homicidal-maniac Alan Winterbourne tucked away under spud guns, an instructional essay to restudy in case the shit ever hits the fan, or in case we'd like it to. Of course, Winterbourne, whose last job before an eight-year losing streak was a secret missile project at the Northrop Corporation that unsteadied his soul and mind, was far removed from the frappaccino-sipping HTML-flipping South Park scene we're so fond of lamenting. If Alan had only held on a few more years, might he have found an appropriate outlet for his hostilities on, um, Heat.net?

"Soylent Green is people!" —*Charlton Heston*, Soylent Green

THE computer industry eats people, consumes them whole, and spits out bleached-white bones. While corpulent, sickly white prepublic CEOs masturbate over their vested stock, their lackeys, their Dockers-and-button-down-clad minions, push and push and push the people who do the actual work until stomachs writhe in acid and sleep disappears and skin goes bad and teeth ache. The people who do the actual work rarely push back. Instead they snap. They freak out and they crumble like a freeway in an earthquake.

If only they could manage to crush those who are just along for the ride.

This industry is sick, sick to the core. Apps, games, the web, all of it. People who work eight hours a day then go home to families and lives are derided as not being "**team players.**" People who throw themselves into criminally unreasonable lumber-mill schedules (part buzzsaw, part logjam) are rewarded with more work. People who point all this out are threatened with the loss of their jobs and labeled attitude problems.

If you think the blatant greed and stupidity that Wall Street has demonstrated where tech stocks are concerned is disgusting, try sneaking into the boardroom or CEO's office of a company about to go public. From the cubes in Development, you can hear oily hands being rubbed together and fat, dripping tongues smacking wet lips, just waiting for the cash to rain out of the sky. Human costs aren't considered, families don't

"Downward Mobility," by Denes House
http://arachnid.colgate.edu/intervarsity/
Articles/Downward.html
Feeling uninspired? Working alongside cretins for virtual cash got you down? Perhaps the motivational parting thoughts given to some graduating high school seniors by Colgate University Christian Fellowship instructor Denes House could raise your spirits. "Jesus' philosophy is one of downward mobility," House explains, finding the genesis of the concept of toil in Genesis 3:14-19. And while it's always a pick-me-up to compare one's occupational woes to those of a pin-and-mounted contrarian, at least He got to enjoy throwing the moneylenders out of the temple. You, on the other, are one paycheck away from a bargain flyaway weekend in Vegas. Examine your conscience. Now get back to work.

exist, there is no Outside (only, perhaps, *Outside*). "Tell them they have to work weekends," the boss says to his winged monkey. "Tell them that they're not working hard enough."

And the winged monkey, just to show you what a wonderful guy he is, offers to buy you a burrito and a Coke because you're missing dinner at home. Gosh, Brad, thanks.

The days when it was worth it are over. There used to be a time, long ago, when killing yourself for the company was worth it. I believe that. I read *Hackers* and *Show-stopper!* and fell for it, fell for it hard. I believed that you could eat shit and say it was porridge for a few years and come out of it with a huge number of neurons fried, but with enough lucre in the bank that you could spend the rest of your life working it out in a hillside bunker (or, better yet, a yurt filled with high-tech toys).

But that doesn't happen anymore. Kill yourself now and the only thing you are is dead, and all you'll get is a gold-plated coffin. For the people who can make it through the entire vesting period, the shares almost never add up to anything significant: yes, yours for just the cost of four years of your life – friends, sex, contentment, peace, and an apartment free of that sickly smell it gets when you haven't been there in a long time – a new car!

The 500 Point Nerdity Test

http://www.armory.com/tests/nerd500 .html

Nerds haven't just programmed themselves into the top of the social strata; they're assimilating like crazy. Ample evidence of this can be found in the Nerdity Test, a 1993 document which seems just a tad more useful today than the average phrenology chart. The general Knowledge section still has the power to gloss the eyes of the nondweeb, with its questions on Maxwell's equations and spherical harmonic functions. But the extensive Computers section is, at best, a quaint anachronism, with its questions on the now-ubiquitous knowledge of .sig files, multitasking, and telnet clients. By the time you reach question #432 ("Was the last naked person you saw a hi-res scan?"), you might be struck with the sinking feeling that you're already a winner, whether you like it or not.

Whoop-de-fuckin'-do. The equivalent of, what? A 10 percent raise? At the cost of a stomach lining? A decent night's sleep? A full head of hair? A life?

Never before in history have **nerds,** as a class, become economically viable. It was never worthwhile to exploit astronomers. But computer programmers can actually make something people want, something people will pay for. And they overfocus anyway! Convince them that The Product is somehow important to their lives, more important than their lives, and hang a turd from a stick and call it a carrot. And bang! Coding machines! *Machines* being the operative word.

It's sick and it's immoral. A friend of mine was beeped to work – he had to carry a beeper – on a weekend, on his wife's birthday, and he didn't return home until 2 A.M. The videogame he was working on had a bug. The videogame. The manager who called him in probably got a raise.

Something is desperately wrong, wrong and evil. Butchers and bakers and candlestick makers don't have to put up with this kind of shit, so why should we? Why is it expected? Demanded? Why is it given? Why is an eight-hour day a "good start"? When did the job become the end instead of the means? Why should I make that evil bastard in the corner office rich? Why should he get a million dollars for the product I architected? For my product? The product he's too stupid to understand?

Because that's the way it is. Fine. At least I don't have to watch.

I quit.

Sub-Middle Management Worksick Blues

by Lotte Absence

I thought I knew how to negotiate bureaucracies – how to sidestep the George Romero zombies of middle management who aren't comfortable unless they have a meeting to decide when the next silt-deposit-paced meeting is going to take place.

Well, I was wrong.

Did anyone expect the web "industry" to be any different than, say, the movie industry or the music industry? Vanity, corruption of power, insecurities, neuroses, unprofessionalism, and flat-out back-stabbing have all shown their ugly head in this nascent enterprise – and perhaps that's the surest sign that the web baby will reach maturity . . . if it doesn't drown in its own filth first, of course.

"Payback's the thing you gotta see," said James Brown, and the time is nigh for a little payback to the weasels of the web. If there were such a thing as a web industry veteran, I think I would qualify. I've got two start-up sites under my belt since 1994. I've worked for little companies that became big, big companies that wanted to think small, and big companies run by small people.

Most recently, I tangled with the latter animal; I was hired to create a site aimed at the eighteen to thirty-five demographic. As a director (at least in title), I recruited talent, did conceptual brainstorming, and code-veloped a business/operating plan.

We created a budget for equipment and employees, and while it was too high, it wasn't sent back for revision. After one of countless reorgs, it simply disappeared.

Months went by. Finally, we sent out a distress signal to the Land of Middle Management Zombies. "Please help us navigate the bureaucratic shoals and political riptides of this corporate behemoth," we said. And from Central Zombie Casting, they sent us a Seasoned Zombie Pol. A slick and resilient lifer from the hallowed halls of the parent company, he came coated in Teflon and bearing holsters full of Pam. Hopes were raised, fears allayed – the Seasoned Zombie Pol would act as "business manager" and help us finesse the budgetary dollars we needed, and push our agenda in the halls of the top management bots.

Once all the talent (writers, production artists, editors) was pushed through the molasses-slow hiring process (as employment offers were known to sit on desks for weeks at a time, trying to get someone hired was on par with squeezing Pamela Anderson Lee into her swimsuit – slow going, but worth it . . .), we were able to deliver an impressive prototype in less than a month. But, as is the case sometimes with young, hastily assembled teams, we slowed down.

There were still deadlines, but they were seldom observed, because the launch date was never etched in stone. A placeholder launch date kept getting pushed back, as the head of the project got cold feet about committing to a firm date. Morale was plummeting. Something had to happen. So I pushed for a shuffle of editorial management positions. It seemed like the only answer.

A firm date was set, and the crew felt relieved to know where they stood. The site launched on time, and while not perfect, things did look bright. But a funny thing happened on the way to the circus. Our new editorial management staff chose to spend countless hours in a tautological feedback loop – checking out what was being said about them and defending themselves against critics on popular online forums of discus-

sion. Patting themselves on the back, bragging loudly, slagging other websites, and defending their work on a daily basis, while investing minimal work to improve our site – it became yet another example of a generational tendency toward instant gratification and solipsistic discourse.

Now, I have nothing against spending time online. Online discussion can be a valuable marketplace for exchanging thoughts and ideas with peers. But when the balance of hours tips away from creating actual online work, and toward strutting, puffing, and clucking about said work in online forums, well that's when it's time for some egos to check themselves, because the competition is real – and cheap, personal vanity is as common as zip codes.

Below me, I wanted to steer the technology of the site with a team of programmers and coders. Before launch, I tried to organize and set goals for the team. But I was unpleasantly surprised by the some of the responses of a few twenty-something hotshot webmeisters (at that time working on freelance contract) to the request of actually doing work. They refused on occasion, and sometimes threatened work stoppages if not paid faster than "Net 30."

Nothing can age you faster than seeing how babies behave, and the arrogance these kids showed – not so much helpless as willfully lazy – is rare among those already out of diapers. It was difficult to believe that kind of work ethic could put one anywhere else but in a nursery or the unemployment line. Still, with the current fluidity of the web job market, young webmeisters know that they can go elsewhere. Coming in at 2 P.M. and working hard until 11 P.M. has never bothered me. Coming in and refusing to do the work assigned, while playing videogames, web surfing, or chatting in a Palace site . . . well, I guess a DreamJob is one you can wear your Pampers to.

Meanwhile, the Zombie Pol "business manager" started riding this project like it was Jenny McCarthy, or like he was Jenny McCarthy riding a subtsunami PR wave. However you work it out, it worked for him. The zombie's association with the site's (initial) success gave him new life in the eyes of the company. Though the mere prevalence of best-selling management books that talk about the dangers of being a "control freak" or a "micromanager" doesn't mean much, there are times when common sense burbles through even the granite of an MBA. Still, micromanage is exactly what the Zombie decided to do. It's an undead thing, I guess.

After I was relieved of all my authority and agency, I decided to leave the project. It's little comfort to know that the project is floundering still. (They actually expect it to make money next year!) It has also been victim to the whim of corporate belt-tightening budget cuts. But this does not change the overarching fact that to have one's name associated with something less than a team's best effort is no honor and of even less value.

In my gut, I know that if I decided to leave the industry right now, and come back in two years, it would be a lot easier. Sure, the technology would have improved dramatically, but more importantly, the **fucking business model** would have been figured out by then. Websites, done on a large scale, are expensive propositions, and no one's really making money doing them. Nevertheless, when a site is mismanaged (and by inseparable extension, the staff of a site is mismanaged), it doesn't matter how much money is thrown at the goal – it's going to be second-rate. For some companies, that's good enough. But no one says you have to work for them.

"Make Relationships, Not Money, On The Web"
http://www.zdnet.com/intweek/print/
960708/attitude/col2.html
Nick Routledge, writing for *Inter@active Week,* sees in the web a business model that may be intrinsically uneconomical, even in the long term. "In a context where the cost of information distribution is essentially nil," Routledge opines, "charging consumers for an experience that engages them most effectively makes no sense, because it's an approach that represents nothing less than charging for the right to extend your influence." While true for fledgling brands, this analysis is less relevant to outfits like ESPN Sportzone, whose influence is vast enough to warrant US$1 daily fees from its users, or the online version of the *Wall Street Journal,* which has not failed miserably with its subscription model. Call it the "Gravy Theory": The secret to online success is not needing to succeed online. If you do happen to rake in some bucks – well, that's just gravy.

Nite Crawler

by Justine

PAST 2 A.M., raining. There was no one to email, no one to talk to, simply the company of my own indwelling self-doubt monsters and longings ill-becoming my station. What there was, was to hit AltaVista and get into trouble.

Of course, I wanted to trick the machine, skeptical it could do anything for me. I gave it a string that I was sure it couldn't find, that of my Great Lost Love (elsewhere referred to as Dirk Van Hooeven, whose absence is always present, much like the redshift of receding stars). I typed in Dirk's name and waited for AltaVista to stall. As far as I knew, Dirk, a high-ranking officer in the cabals of global finance, had nothing to do with the net landgrab or the silliness of personal web pages or anything tasteless or technologically off-point, ever.

But the infernal machine came up with nine matches – my jaw would have dropped if there had been a human interpreter to see it.

Ghost traces of Dirk in HTML, he existed in the form of portfolio-management conference proceedings, official bios, and agendas. Business-to-business marketing on the web had placed him within my grasp for sicko late-night lonesome cowgirl inspections.

And if I wanted to, right then and there in the privacy of my own home, I could have ordered a two-hour tape of Dirk talking – about the latest in barely legal financial chicanery, no doubt. No matter. For only US$30 I could have delivered by snail mail, in plain brown businessy wrapping, his patented chesty rumble that had always made me go mush. I thought about making the purchase – but I couldn't do it.

Too humiliating, too akin to my feeling about sex toys – sad and shoddy phantasms of Genuine Contact.

I scanned the rest of the listings. I could tell he'd moved back to New York from L.A., changed jobs. If I wanted to, I could now call him at his to-me new Manhattan office and say, "Hey, Dirk, 'play Misty for me'!"

I logged off, aghast. I hadn't meant to, yet in using AltaVista I had become a snoop, stalking Dirk online. And I knew that from now on, I would probably be able to trace his whereabouts, his career – better and faster and cheaper than the use of any private detective. Unless Dirk ceased from being a financial double-alpha, as Business went more and more online, it would be easier and easier to be up-to-date on his life.

I had done something really sickening.

Nevertheless I couldn't help myself – having seen what AltaVista could do with Dirk, who didn't really belong in cyberspace, I wanted to see what it would do with Wretch, who did.

Wretch, my first date in two years and head technologist for an entertainment combine (call it FlameBoyCo). Wretch was much inclined to giving good quote about better business practices on the Net. And while nothing had ever really happened between me and Wretch, like a splinter under the skin, he was a foreign body my system of psychoneuro-immunology was taking a long time to dissolve.

Since Wretch, unlike Dirk, did have a vanilla, probably-would-score-web-hits-in-the-thousands kinda name – let's say "Charles Forbes" – I did a search on "Charles Forbes and FlameBoy."

Sure enough, AltaVista was happy to show me Wretch – sounding like his usual charismatic/flake self. I could just imagine his intonations, his moues, his practiced aw-shucks-knock-'em-dead force, as I read the transcript of a radio interview with him and another net business expert guy. It brought Wretch back vividly – a shameful flare-up of the infatuation I had tamped down months before.

Still, I was into it; I had to go for it.

I reengaged with the accursed AltaVista and called up his listings again. And then the strangest damned thing happened: I was directed to a bunch of queer websites. Huh? I skimmed them with increasing dismay – until I ran across the mention of the outing of Forbes and FlameBoy. FlameBoy, the eponymous founder of the company Wretch worked for, was famously gay in Hollywood.

I logged off again. Was that what it had been? That Wretch – in spite of his statements ("I'm not gay") and actions (bragging about how much money he made had appeared to be a ty-pi-cal Regular Guy display to impress a female he wanted to bed) to the contrary – was gay? I'd had reasons to wonder, and it would be much nicer to ascribe his herky-jerky/hot-cold behavior to sexual indeterminacy. Better a closet case than (as a friend said) "a lovely turd."

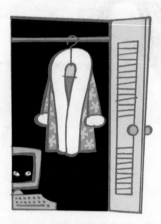

I thought about what had the look and feel of an unwanted discovery. At the very least, it didn't seem right that the web should be the means for outing a former potential object of desire.

I sat at my computer, motionless, the screen still carrying evidence of this latest adventure in data mining, apparently so incriminating of Wretch. Nauseated at what could be retrieved by anyone about anyone, or what could appear to be retrieved, totally thrown by what it seemed I had come across (being lied to, a closet life). Then it came to me: Alta-Vista in its machine literal-mindedness had approximated my Charles Forbes with the outed Malcolm Forbes (a close, not exact, match).

And though I was able to salvage my mate-hunting *amor-propre* (and maintain the historic good hit-rate of my hyper-sensitive Martian perceptual apparati), I remained disturbed that it was so easy to have drawn the wrong conclusions, extracted the wrong "information," done research assumed to be correct because done by computer – when because of the ways humans fill in the spaces in between, it was wrong.

With some relief, Wretch slipped back into the category I had constructed for him with much will and reluctance months before – like the Doubtful Case in Camus's *The Plague*, Wretch remained ambivalent for damned sure, but probably not about the gender of those he wanted to toy with.

By 4 A.M., I finally finished my network antics, after trying out the name of my ex-husband, the name of the second guy I'd slept with (a draft dodger I had fallen in love with when I had been a fifteen-year-old runaway), and the first of my smooth-talking good-looking SOBs (an erratically brilliant CalTech undergrad who had gone down in history as my first encounter with my weakness for polymath sociopaths). Thank goddess none of them were there.

And Dirk wouldn't know, and Wretch wouldn't know, that I had been sidling up to them for hours.

Yet when I logged out for the last time, I was afraid of email that might await me from Wretch or Dirk. Somehow, through the genius of magical thinking, my scare at getting caught led me to fear they might link back to me through my linking to their names on the Web.

The guilt about acting furtive was about as rational as the atavistic fear of contagion that erupted as I had held the hand of my best friend as he lay dying of AIDS in San Francisco General Ward 5A. Though I knew better, I had still gotten tested a few months later. So it was with assuming my lost subjects-for-limerance would be able to tell I had been pawing at them electronically, like an opossum or chipmunk scrabbling through papers on their desks. I was afraid of little track marks or scuffles, signs of (tele)presence.

It had become clear even before the sun came up that I could be updated on the World Wide Web life of Dirk and Wretch as each week AltaVista enhanced and refreshed itself. And I knew I would not do it. The gesture was sneaky and unclean. Unrequited love should more honorably be left where it's always belonged: in the body – the head and the heart – and not in discorporated electronic pulses of intelligent agents – of those who pine.

POP CULT FOLLOWING

Coke Coke Coke Coke Coke Coke Coke Coke Coke Coke Coke Coke Coke Coke Coke

People complain
about the state of
American popular culture as
though it were a problem that couldn't be
solved, yet solutions are posed every day: television definition
so clear it defeats its mind-numbing purpose; enough channels
to wear calluses on all ten fingers; scads of webzines and print
zines whose very motivation is to turn unexploited trends into
clichés. To be sure, there is something deeply unnerving about
a nation that can support both *Extreme Championship*

Wrestling and *Party of Five* in equivalent proportions – but also deeply exhilarating as well. If there is something wrong with American popular culture, it's that we haven't figured out how to criticize it in a way that's as entertaining as the subject itself.

Unfortunately, embracing the idea of American popular culture is altogether easier than embracing its actual products – especially since the slow congelation of media companies into a thick, world-spanning agar tends to suspend everything, from the lowest common denominator on up, at eye-level. Indeed, satellite television, transnational entertainment conglomerates, and round-the-world, round-the-clock "news" have homogenized birthday wishes and conspiracy theories from Oakland to Osaka, setting the stage for both unprecedented levels of consensual paranoia and David Hasselhoff's international music career. In the '80s, proponents of the global village promised a borderless, buffet-style approach to identity, but a few years into the new world order, dinner looks less like a multiculti appetizer plate and more like a Happy Meal.

EUROTRASHED
page 114

A CROSS-EYED BETWEEN
page 117

Which explains why E. L. Skinner is concerned, though not really alarmed, about the infiltration of European-style foodstuff and beverages ("'handcrafted' beer and boutique bread") into American culture ("Since when are Budweiser and Wonderbread not good enough for Americans?"). What saves us from recolonization, he explains in "Eurotrashed," is that cultural imports are the hallmark of a civilization successful enough to buy its way out of cultural debt. Seymour Cranium speculates on a different kind of creative hybridization in "A Cross-Eyed Between": "You're automatically something new if you're a mix of two things that no one ever thought of mixing before."

ANYWHERE, USA
page 128

Nowhere has this "you've got your chocolate in my peanut butter" approach to marketing worked more successfully than with the chain-bookstore-cum-social centers of Barnes & Noble and Borders. Miss de Winter's examination of "Anywhere, USA" finds that these companies are simply capitalizing on a general trend to turn stores into "shopping destinations," where the craving for community "can be fulfilled without compromising our need for convenience." One-stop community building is also the subject of Ann O'Tate's "The Fire This Time," a rumination on the Burning Man Festival, whose gleefully destructive neo-paganism finds an analog on the other side of the globe; only there, the self-immolations are real.

WIGGED OUT
page 120

THE FIRE THIS TIME
page 132

The white light/white heat generated by the explosion of celebrities on to the entertainment radar gets examined by Ersatz in "Wigged Out" – a reevaluation of the shadow cast by the consummate sell-out, Andy Warhol, especially as refracted through numerous cinematic attempts to make a star out of the inventor of Super-Stardom. In light of his essay, one may wonder not whether David Bowie's turn as the Polish Pop Art Prince in *Basquiat* helps or hurts the Thin White Duke's star power, but, as Johnny Cache might ask, whether it raised his yield. In "To Market, To Market," Johnny Cache uses David Bowie's Wall Street debut as the Merrill-Lynch-pin of a proposal to turn celebrity into a true public asset. Helpful for prospective investors, Cleary S. Day's "An Astral Theory of Rock" charts the cosmology of this economic universe, annotating the five-step life cycle of a star: Birth, Radiation, Exhaustion, Collapse, and Black Hole. "How far the star collapses, and into what kind of object – VH1 spokesperson, singer of country tunes in odd time signatures, role in the touring company of *Grease* – is determined by the star's final mass."

TO MARKET,
TO MARKET
page 110

AN ASTRAL
THEORY OF
ROCK
page 124

But one should be wary of mathematical approaches to cultural analysis. As mentioned, the tendency towards global cultural equilibrium makes weighing pop products a tricky proposition, and makes judging their value well-nigh impossible. While the sheer ubiquity of American symbols and shows does suggest we've won the global culture war, one should be careful not to confuse mass with meaning. American popular culture travels easiest across borders because our language of signs and slogans is the closest this modern world still has to the sublingual; in a post-literate age, we've shown ourselves the most adept at communicating in grunts.

To Market, To Market

by Johnny Cache

HE'S not a doctor, but he played one on TV. And even if his rerun fees haven't put him on the back nine, the experience still keeps him in the black. These days, former *M*A*S*H* star Wayne Rogers applies poultices to hemorrhaging bank accounts in his new role – as a financial adviser to the stars. Specializing in the problems endemic to monumental, undeserved wealth, Trapper John, MBA, recently explained his management philosophy to *People*: "Celebrities are businesses . . . Burt Reynolds is an asset."

Perhaps you hadn't ever thought of The Bandit quite that way. But the truism that celebrities are commodities is no longer just a clever line – it's the bottom one. February saw the enormously successful public offering of interest-bearing David Bowie bonds.

The deal went down something like this: The Thin White Duke was craving cash, and he saw that while on paper he was rich, his net worth was all tied up in future record royalties. So as musicians often do when they need money, he decided to tour. What was different was that he decided to tour Wall Street.

There he and his band of financiers trotted out hit number after hit number: balance sheets, cash flow statements, and projected revenue based on the Bowie franchise's past operating performance. The Street thought it recognized a good gamble; they would issue interest-bearing bonds with Bowie's royalties as collateral. He would get paid up front; they would get to be in the music business. And the bonds, each representing a share of Mr. Ziggy Stardust, would trade on the open market, like orange juice, pork bellies, or Intel.

At least in theory they would. In reality, only a few **select institutional scalpers,** like Prudential, got a piece of the rock star. Bowie, meanwhile, probably entertained more people with his financial prowess (he made over US$50 million) than with his latest public musical offering, which peaked at an underwhelming thirty-nine on the music charts.

The market for this new kind of personal finance – or "personnel finance" – starts with an AAA star like Bowie. But its expansion into B-rated and junk bonds is as close to a sure thing as you'll see on Wall Street. David Bowie today means Dave Matthews and Dave Barry tomorrow.

It's not so unreasonable. You go to a movie, you watch some unknown actor steal a few scenes, you walk out with a hunch he's gonna hit the big time. You can talk about him at the water cooler, or you can put your money where your mouth is, and buy shares of his stock. If you find out he hasn't gone public yet, all the better. It probably means he's

"The Buck Starts Here," by Ken Kurson (July 8, 1996)
http://www.tripod.com/work/columns/ kurson/960708.html
Ken Kurson is one of the vanguard of young entrepreneurs who have set out to make a buck by teaching people to make a buck. What's different about Ken's approach is that it's both legal and (not yet) an infomercial. Actually, he's making the money the old-fashioned way, by profiting on the ignorance of others, specifically, that of young people who until recently probably regarded mutual funds and IRA accounts as morally equivalent to major label recording contracts and McDonald's. Ken's presence on the Tripod site – a suite of programming aimed specifically at "Gen X" – proves not so much that money is cool, but that it always has been. It's Gen X that goes in and out of style.

still waiting tables and would welcome your venture capital. Five hundred bucks on Matthew McConaughey at Dazed and Confused prices could be worth over fifty Gs today.

The possibilities, as usual, are endless. Take the billions in allowance money that's just hanging out – the teenage-capital market is hugely underpenetrated. What better way to get that cash working than a Billboard Top 40 Mutual Fund? It could pay dividends in Tower Records gift certificates. The kids would love it.

Or: The first one hundred thousand copies of the new U2 disc could come with a few shares of common stock, turning a frivolous entertainment expense into a good, sound investment. All it would take is a few fans on Motley Fool touting UTWO as a fabulous growth stock and the CD would pay for itself in days.

The only thing really separating The Hollywood Stock Exchange and E*Trade is our faith that Merrill Lynch's ability to package a winner is greater than CAA's. Who knows how long that will last. All that's missing is the appropriate news organ to pump out summaries of the trading day's activity – a *Wall Street Variety Journal*. "Dark-horse Oscar nominee Bill Macy up 1-1/8," reports the front page; "much-hyped Paglia stock off a fraction, and shares of Madeline Albright unchanged on news of her being a Jew."

Fame and entertainment have become more about money – another truism. But money has of late itself become so much more entertaining. It probably has as much to do with start-ups throwing options around like Monopoly scrip as any genuinely rising interest in, well, rising interest. But whatever the cause, making money suddenly seems less like work and more like a game. Or at least that's what Dow Jones and ITT, which launched New York's WBIS+, would like you to think. The television channel throws together the stuff guys like, in the order they like it: "Sports, Money, and oh yeah, Life."

It's bound to succeed. Exhibit A: **OJ-2.** Was not this model of BIS+'s conflation (not to say confusion) of real life with finance and football a smash hit? The only strange part is that though the second trial seemed to be a product of the entertainment industry, it actually came out of the court system. (But then, these have been swapping fluids lately, too.) It was both a three-ring circus and a product-liability suit. Guilty of murder? No – but responsible for wrongful deaths, by all means. There was a serious flaw in the Simpson product for which the parent company, O. J. Simpson, will be made to pay. Sadly, he doesn't have the cash.

Now, he could go bankrupt. Many of the best celebrities do.

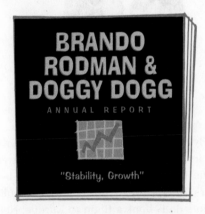

But is this a man with no profit potential? Of course not, and that's why we expect the more logical move from the Juice: an IPO. With wrongful-death compatriot Philip Morris trading at seventeen times earnings, it's an easy play to call. Seventeen times, say, US$5 million in film and book rights, and the not-guiltiest man in showbiz would be sitting on over US$80 megs in stock. He could pay off the over US$30 million in lawsuits, cover the tax bill, and still have a not-uncomfortable seven-figure bank account – offshore, of course. Granted he'd have to sell a controlling interest in himself to realize that much profit. But then it's already clear that the one person who shouldn't be running O. J. Simpson Inc. is O. J. Simpson. His talents lie elsewhere.

So when you hear that the Juice is having himself genetically replicated, don't think of it as cloning. Think of it as a two-for-one split.

Eurotrashed

by E. L. Skinner

***Mutant Food, from* The Happy Mutant's Handbook**

http://www.nathan.com/projects/mutant.html

Better living through household chemicals. The Happy Mutant's approach to cultural perversity is reverse-alterna-retro hip: serving suggestions include Wonderbread Sushi ("Spread the fillings of your choice along the top, leaving a border. Next, roll the bread into a Ho-Ho shape and slice into 3/4" sections.") and The Convenience Food Party, where "ONLY brand names are allowed . . . Chex Mix, Cheese Puffs, and anything else ending with a ™ or ® is ideal." Embrace the mainstream hard enough, the handbook suggests, and you might extrude a turd of creative deviance.

THERE was a period – not coincidentally, around the time of the second OPEC energy crisis – when Monty Python's Flying Circus was about the only European import we ever saw. Sports cars, classical recordings, and tacos were the only products we Americans had to remind us there might be a larger world beyond our borders. But the go-go '80s made a lot of idiots rich, and the first thing rich idiots do is book a flight to Europe. Not long after that, those annoying triangular candy bars started infiltrating our beloved strip malls.

Perhaps it was an inadvertent coming-of-age. Today, we're not only overwhelmed by European products from Nutella to Range Rovers – we're actually being colonized on a cultural level. How else to explain the sudden spectacular popularity of absurdly un-American products like "handcrafted" beer and boutique bread? <u>Since when are Budweiser</u> and Wonderbread not good enough for Americans?

Organic spelt baguettes and honey-weiss beer are expanding nicely in the market niche that muesli was able to boldly chip out of the monolithic American pantry back in the '80s. And who can argue with the apparently rediscovered aesthetic of quality? Who (besides the vast majority of middle-class Americans who aren't burdened with good taste) would actually prefer a can of beer to a bottle of ale? The problem, though, is that all formulas are susceptible to counterfeit or co-optation. Hence Coors licenses "Killian's Red," Kraft invents "DiGiorno Tortellini," and Nabisco spreads the "Grey Poupon." These are great American com-

panies. They ought to be proud to just keep pumping out the hot dogs, root beer, and antacid tablets.

That's not the worst of it. The one thing that created a consensus in America, the single most common reason to get out of bed in the morning – coffee – has been forever spoiled by Starbucks-style upscaling that smacks of European pretensions. Fifteen years ago, who'd ever heard of "espresso"? Even the hippest cosmopolitan coffeehouses (a decade ago, a "cafe" was a rural diner) used to unabashedly advertise "expresso" with a great big foolish American grin. "It's just real, real strong coffee in a little cup" was the mantra long before scones made their crumbly North American debut.

Indeed, with the universal age of consent inching upward, it would seem there are plenty of young Americans who need a place to legally hang out. Where idle eighteen-year-olds used to be able to drink them-selves into a stupor at the bar, now they can sip themselves into apoplexy at the cafe. The upscaling that turned a "Cuppa Joe" into a "Double

Latte" couldn't have come at a more opportune moment. And what a terrifically quaint, European thing to do: hang out in the local coffee shop controverting radical politics. Or at least look like it.

There's proof everywhere you go. And don't think our American institutions – like baseball, Mom, and apple pie – are invulnerable. In recent weeks, Newsweek and others have published polls on the presidential campaign that actually include a demographic category made up of "soccer moms." Soccer moms. Who really believes that this dubious European graft could actually prove to be the swing vote?

A quick glance at a Pottery Barn catalog will show you just how far we've come in trying to reproduce Europe's dilapidated infrastructure, too. Taking their cue from the photographs of Jan Saudek and postgraduate pilgrimages to Prague, upscale condo developers, architects, and decorators across the land are trying to make their properties look like peeling, pooped-out bomb shelters.

Why stop with the walls? A hundred years ago, Americans were embarrassed that we didn't have any civil history in the form of monumental ruins like the Parthenon or Stonehenge. Today, we've simply put our food and home furnishing industries to work redesigning the props of American life to look old and comfortable . . . just like what they have over in the Old World. You know, like France. Because you're an American, you don't actually have a history. But you can afford to buy one. Henry Ford would be proud.

A Cross-Eyed Between

by Seymour Cranium

CADILLACS used to be found on both drive-
ways and desktops. Pre-Accord,
you could assert the superiority of anything – say, a stapler – by announc-
ing it as the "Cadillac of staplers." In 1996 only Cadillacs are called
Cadillacs, as nobody wants to evoke the image of struggling to find new
appeal now that one's traditional customer base is dying off. Besides, in
many cases the metaphor is no longer apt; staplers don't have half the
desk-hugging weight that they used to. (Considering that desks don't
have half the weight they used to, this is probably a good thing.)

Given the Cadillac's current position, it's easy to forget there was
a time when country club parking lots were filled with nothing else. But

Cadillac, the brand name, was already on the skids in the late '70s. It's no accident that the **demise** of the DeVille coincides with Jimmy Carter's diagnosis of "a malaise in the land" – if we didn't have a name for the top of the heap anymore, how could we aspire to it?

Still, nature must not abhor this vacuum so very much, as the sad truth is that no other brand has taken the place of Cadillac as the name for all that is superlative, excessive, and American. No matter; we've graduated to touting things as a cross between two other known quantities. While the Largemouth Bass might simply be a "cross between two species," Diamanda Galas is a cross between "Bela Lugosi and Shirley Bassey."

Hybrid-hype sounds better, anyway – the best of both worlds is always preferable to either world by itself. Plus, you're automatically something new if you're a mix of two things that no one ever thought of mixing before – in this way new math, 1 + 1 = 3! And the more incongruous the two are, the better, as that makes you all the more **outrageous.** What else can explain the description of New Orleans as a "surrealistic cross between Disneyworld and Calcutta"?

The best advantage of all, though, is that a mixed breed doesn't even have to resemble either of its putative progenitors. Calling something a cross is an opportunity to massage the truth so smoothly that no one sees any stretch marks. Kids don't necessarily look just like their parents, after all.

Speaking of kids, consider *XY* magazine, trying to carve out a niche as a lifestyle magazine for gay youths. The front cover of the third issue tells us it's "[a] cross between *Details* and *Wired* for young gay men." Sounds like a winner already – those magazines sell lots of copies, don't they? But wait, what sorts of features would you expect in a magazine spawned by *Wired*? An attempt at trenchant commentary on life at the dawn of the digital age? No, but *XY* has plenty of photos. All manner

of color? Nope – half the pages in *XY* are black and white, for goodness' sake. An advertiser-enticing affluent readership? Well, depends on whether or not the readership is actually "young gay men," or if *XY* is simply *Barely Legal* in chaps. But not to worry – it's no problem if you've hitched your wagon to a star with the most tenuous of threads. The scam is painless when you say you're a hybrid. After all, maybe there's truth in *XY* being something like *Details*.

It helps that no one expects anything resembling truth in advertising. All the seventeen-inch monitors measure sixteen inches (diagonally), and no one could care less. Two-by-fours aren't. Most SLR camera lenses have a somewhat smaller aperture than their spec. But, the photo mags remind us, "They're all within accepted industry tolerances." Sure – and just coincidentally all on the minus side, yes? Technology-intensive consumer goods have created an unprecedented opportunity for sellers to fudge the descriptions of their wares. What consumer is going to check if their new 6x CD-ROM drive really spins at 6x? How many even know what it's supposed to be running six times as fast as, anyway? Not that retailers – or pundits, for that matter – know any better. Those who get their technical information about device speeds from *The New York Times* are in big trouble. The "Personal Computers" column recently "explained" that a millisecond is one millionth of a second. (That darn **metric** system is so confusing.)

The worst thing about most fudged specs isn't even that they're dishonest, but – whether they be measured crossways or merely cross-referenced – that they're so boring. It doesn't take twenty-eight grams of creativity to lie about a number. On the other hand, there's an art to finessing the issue by transcending specs altogether. One can't help but appreciate the wry humor in Rolls-Royce exempting itself from plebeian pissing contests, saying only that the horsepower of its car engines is "sufficient." At your next job interview (the one where they want you to be a cross between Sisyphus and Horatio Alger) give that answer when they ask for your salary requirement. And the quality of your work? It's within accepted industry tolerances.

The National Institute of Technology and Standards Metric Program Pages
http://ts.nist.gov/ts/htdocs/200/202/mpo_home.htm

There's something comforting about artifacts from the '70s, like, say, Keith Richards, that refuse to die. While you might not know about the National Institute of Technology and Standards, much less its "Metric Outreach Activities" (be sure to take place in a "Regional Metric Dialog" when it comes to your town!), the institute knows about you. What's more, it knows you don't care. The transcript from the 1995 Metric Town Meeting in Atlanta offers faint hope for the beleaguered measurement system, pinning its future on a combination of the Clinton administration's benign neglect ("Maybe this is a blessing in disguise since metric conversion is always a target for demagoguery and making fun") and a touching faith in the youth of today: "The younger Federal managers want to go metric. I'm not sure what the explanation for this is. Perhaps because they're a different generation they want to do something different for their generation." Still, all is not lost – pointy-headed as they may be, these government bureaucrats realize that their quixotic campaign to help America out of the English System ghetto (where its only neighbors are Myanmar and Liberia) lacks only a catchy slogan to break wide. As another attendant of the Atlanta meeting noted, "It sounds as though it was a Nike advertisement here, 'Just do it.' Right?"

Wigged Out

by Ersatz

WILL the movies ever get Andy Warhol right? Don't hold your breath – at least not longer than fourteen minutes, fifty-nine seconds.

Now, only a fool expects to get turned on to visual art by Hollywood. But given that painting makes Page One only when it involves forgery, defacement, theft, embezzlement, or a US$75 coffee-table book, the art world could use a celluloid plug.

Of course, Warhol isn't the only dauber ever to get an unfair screen shake. The typical movie artist is Nick Nolte in *New York Stories:* tortured by Morrissey-grade angst, drinking W. C. Fields-worthy thermoses of Scotch, and tossing enough paint for two barns on a sail-sized canvas (all while renting a loft so big that real estate agents would require Paul Allen to have Bill Gates sign on as guarantor). And Anthony Hopkins bared his barrel chest and treated his lovers like dirt in *Picasso*, probably the only name as popularly synonymous with sadism as Hannibal Lecter.

But Warhol's signature images (packaging, icons, disasters, portraits) and signature fashions (fright wig, sunglasses, leather, Polaroid) have left him more than usually open to the cheap camera shot. It does not help that his compulsive self-styling makes Dan Rather seem unaffected.

Taking it from the bottom: Robert Zemeckis's 1992 flop *Death Becomes Her.* This dismal Hawn/Streep/Willis vehicle doesn't warrant much nit-picking, but the film's pervasive, out-of-left-field Warhol theme

only throws more itching powder onto the head-scratching viewer's scalp. Early on, it's whispered that the promiscuous Streep "would attend the opening of an envelope." When that quip was originally directed at Warhol, it was "a drawer." Later, a faux Warhol adorns the wall as an undertaker strangles his wife. And in the (none too) climactic scene, Willis squeezes through a crowd of champagne-guzzling undead, backing into Andy – natch – who gulps befuddledly while Monroe whispers in his ear.

To Zemeckis, the very persona of Warhol is a sight gag. Andy's own presence in a few TV ads confirms that most of the time, his image is used as a comic-book turn on "artist." He also did a *Love Boat* episode and surfaces in *Tootsie*, where a brief montage with Andy signifies that Dustin-in-drag has arrived.

Next up: that Oliver Stone guy and *The Doors*, a movie even more dated than its 1991 timestamp would suggest. Kilmer gets led badly astray by the "vampires" of The Factory, improbably dominated by a giant Roy Lichtenstein image. (This is about as likely as John McEnroe mounting a LeRoy Neiman tribute to Jimmy Connors in his SoHo gallery.) Wondering aloud whether "Andy imitates life, or life imitates Andy," a toadlike Capote leads Jim through white light/heat to the inner sanctum. Crispin Glover is sitting under the obligatory wig, which seems to hover.

Stone could plead ignorance for the glib characterization of the man the Velvets dubbed "Drella" (Dracula plus Cinderella). And the Solanas sympathizers behind Jared Harris in *I Shot Andy Warhol* clearly had some gunpowder to grind. But mock-heroic painter Julian Schnabel ought to know better than casting David Bowie as the Wigged One in *Basquiat*. Bowie, who copped his spacey '70s interview style directly from Warhol, can't even shed his British accent. Schnabel garners some points for elegiac treatment of Warhol's senseless death, and shows Andy as genuinely concerned about Basquiat's drugged decline. But this seems mostly a function of Schnabel's melodramatic streak.

Indeed, his self-conscious stylization makes Warhol a hack actor's (or director's) dream. Having tired of the college lecture circuit, he once sent a double in his place. Given that the double was Asian, that the charade took any time at all to unravel suggests that the public's depth perception was as shallow as Andy always gauged it to be. This writer couldn't act his way out of a Woody Harrelson movie, but after watching just a few videos of Warhol's live interviews, he could do as good an Andy as Glover or Harris: "Oh." "Grreeat." "Um, I don't know." "Rrrreally?" Throw in a few references to money, Coca-Cola, and watching a lot of television, and yours truly has a shot at a part in an Edie Sedgwick biopic.

Or so it would seem. No movie has conveyed the humor and bite of Warhol's seemingly dopey routine, especially when pestered by asinine questioners eager to read the worst into his out-of-it facade. Only the 1991 documentary *Superstar* does justice to his Polish roots, and gives a sense of his originality and influence. Dealers, critics, groupies, and Grace Jones all testify to the Death Star tractor beam effect of first exposure to Warhol. The immediate reaction was invariably a huge grin and the question, "What is *that*?"

Peter Schjeldahl, a lone stylist among '80s art critics, acknowledged both the Weighty Import and the pure fun of Warhol. "In the '60s [he] had a steamrollering effect on the whole mental apparatus of Western cultural tradition," Schjeldahl argues. "Warhol wasn't ironic . . . [this was] as efficient a life-form as a shark, a cat, or an honest businessman (which he was)." Explaining the much-derided work of the '70s, he concludes: "American culture simply became so permeated with Warhol's own influence that his responses to it picked up something akin to audio feedback . . . [He] remains way ahead of them, as contemporary civilization's comprehensive visionary." As Warhol would say: "Gosh."

But Schjeldahl doesn't exaggerate; what punk was to bubblegum pop, Pop Art was to the '50s splatter painters. Abstract expressionism

was considered the first wholly American art form, but once Warhol came along with his populist pronouncements ("No one can buy a better Coca-Cola than anyone else") and instant icons, Jackson Pollock and Willem de Kooning began to look pretty darned Parisian. Detractors avoid mentioning that Warhol could draw like a dream, receiving numerous awards for his '50s illustrations. One young illustrator, Jeff Fulvimari, has created a high-profile career for himself by simply duplicating Warhol's '50s blotted-line style. Andy would like that.

Rather than an all-purpose touchstone for all things elitist and flimsy, the man should be a model for egalitarians and aesthetes alike. If pop figures can ever be said to be radical, Warhol is up there with Lenny Bruce, or John Lennon, who said that artists "should do things that the media doesn't understand, because then they can't tear them down." Not that they don't try. All these movies willfully twist Warhol's fresh, contrarian pronouncements ("I want the wrong person for the part," "A computer would make a very qualified boss") into the pap and pomposity he was satirizing. His every move was calculated to undermine notions of the Master inspired by heavenly muses.

Most of all, know-nothing directors have sneered that Warhol "stole" his ideas from other people. Never mind that this ignores and distorts the most basic tenets of appropriation art. Never mind that Warhol made the Duchampian notion of pure selection palatable to the mainstream. If, as they've also suggested, Andy was awash in a sea of motor-mouthed poseurs, he must have been a genius to have fished so many great ideas from such bilgy waters.

He was a media jammer to make Mark Dery green with envy. Wherever he pointed, everything clicked.

An Astral Theory of Rock

by Cleary S. Day

IN the music industry there is life before Soundscan and life after Soundscan. Life on the *Billboard* charts before Soundscan was a prototypical Scorsese movie, dominated by the sleazy triumvirate of radio programmers, record chain executives, and Casey Kasem. Life after Soundscan is blissfully bit-driven, with record sales instantly beamed through the ether from record stores straight to some air-conditioned, Halon gas-protected computer room.

Like any new technology is bound to do, Soundscan has spawned a new job category at every major label – specially trained spreadsheet jocks crunching the raw album sales numbers to tweak market share here, mindshare there, and wallet share everywhere else. Their ultimate goal: maximize the lifetime value of any particular artist.

The result? The Fugees: reconstituted adult rock masquerading as hip-hop.

But I'm going to put all of those data-massaging monkeys out of business. Not with any new harebrained tracking scheme or business model, but with an entirely new methodology of b(r)and scenario planning. Think of it as the place where David Geffen meets Carl Sagan. It's the new Astral Theory of Rock.

During literally days of research, I've discovered that the life cycle of a star mimics that of, well, a star. This flash of brilliance has led me to believe that those Excel worker bees could someday be replaced by a few highly paid quantum physicists, or at least some folks who took Physics for Poets at the local community college. In order to predict the lifetime value of a star, they'll just need to follow the easy-to-remember, five-step life cycle of a true celestial body: Birth, Radiation, Exhaustion, Collapse, Black Hole.

The Birth of the star is easy to predict, and shouldn't concern our new breed of record industry knowledge workers. They should be focused on future record sales, not how the star got there in the first place. All A&R schlepps worth their salt know that some combination of bloodthirsty local fans ("I knew them first!"), sleazy record producers ("Sure, pal. Full creative control. Whatever you say."), and alcoholic managers ("But I landed you your first paying gig, asshole."), mixed together in a crowded, humid club in some godforsaken part of town, usually creates enough pressure and mass to form the infant star. The new science of star tracking, however, will prove that what happens "before" a star is born is irrelevant, since "before" is merely a temporal concept, and has no discernible effect on future record sales.

During most of a star's lifetime, nuclear fusion in the core generates electromagnetic Radiation. In other words, the star just plain shines. The Radiation phase is the most profitable period of a star's life. The highly perceptive star tracker will need to keep tabs on the quantity and quality of a star's shine. Michael Jackson's sequined glove shines. Paul Simon's bald spot shines. Paula Abdul's Lycra™ does not shine. Furthermore, new astronomers should be wary of the "Glistening Effect." Glistening should not be confused with shining. Case in point: Kenny G's saxophone glistens. Michael Bolton's hair shines.

In outer space, a star survives by balancing the outward force of shining with the inward pull of gravity caused by the star's mass. Back in Los Angeles, entertainment physicists should note the "balance of fame" practiced by Madonna, a perpetually radiating star. She always seems to

have an equal number of bodyguards (a show of outward force) and basketball players (an inward pull of gravity) at her beck and call.

If the balance of fame is upset, the star begins the Exhaustion phase. During Exhaustion, the star stops shining, gravitation compresses mass inward, and the star starts feeding on itself. Van Halen is in a prototypical exhaustion phase. The core of the star has contracted (Sammy's out), and it is allowing the remaining nuclear material to be used as fuel (Dave's back, but only for the greatest hits record).

Exhaustion inevitably leads to Collapse. The Collapse phase may last over a period of hundreds of *Entertainment Tonight* segments, during which all remaining fuel is used up. Sting has been in Collapse for years. I've traced the precise beginning of his collapse to the Police song "Mother," which prompted millions of people to learn to accurately program their CD players. How far the star collapses, and into what kind of object (VH1 spokesperson, singer of country tunes in odd time signatures, role in touring company of *Grease*) is determined by the star's final mass and the remaining outward pressure that the burnt-up nuclear residue can muster. Or, in Sting's case, how many jazz musicians he can fit on the head of a pin.

If the star is sufficiently massive, it will collapse into a Black Hole. The rocket scientists among us will immediately recognize the KISS

revival tour as the largest black hole the industry has ever seen. In the center of the black hole lies the singularity (Gene Simmons's tongue), where matter is crushed to infinite density, and the curvature of space-time is extreme. Which explains why millions of people keep expecting to hear "Beth" on the radio and to be reunited with their seventh-grade car pools.

Any twelve-year-old with an Einstein T-shirt can tell you that stars surrounding the Black Hole run the risk of being sucked in. But when the geek with $E=MC^2$ blazened across his hollowed chest happens to be toting an HP 12-C, look out. Because a single Black Hole could suck in an entire star system, creating revenue potential unheard of anywhere else. (Imagine Carl Sagan saying "billions and billions," and you're somewhere in the ballpark.) It's not a coincidence that the KISS tour spawned reunions of Foreigner, Styx, Kansas, the Scorpions, and REO Speedwagon.

Finally, the labels have always struggled with the issue of star retirement. Do they ship them to Vegas? Set them up in rock operas? Or simply send them on some endless talk radio tour? If the Astral Theory proves correct, their problems could be solved. Certain physicists believe that if a star survives the whirling vortex of the black hole, it may find itself in an alternate, parallel universe.

Like Europe.

Anywhere, USA

by Miss de Winter

"Home from Nowhere," by James Howard Kunstler, **The Atlantic Monthly (September 1996)**

http://www.theatlantic.com/atlantic/issues/96sep/kunstler/kunstler.htm

Our love affair with the transient is examined in Kunstler's essay about the literal deterioration of American culture: "We reject the past and the future, and this repudiation is manifest in our graceless constructions. Our residential, commercial, and civic buildings are constructed with the fully conscious expectation that they will disintegrate in a few decades. . . . This process of disconnection from the past and the future, and from the organic patterns of weather and light, done for the sake of expedience, ends up diminishing us spiritually, impoverishing us socially, and degrading the aggregate set of cultural patterns that we call civilization." The tone is eloquent nostalgia (hey, this is the *Atlantic*), and the argument – that our crumbling foundations, physical and otherwise, are a "predictable byproduct of the zoning zeitgeist that deemed shopping and apartment living to be unsuitable neighbors" – seems somewhat conservative (uh, this is the *Atlantic*). But the message is radical: we need to get rid of our cars, stop shopping at the mall, and build neighborhoods that can support a diverse economic and social fabric. Sounds great. Will there be a McDonald's nearby?

THE joke's on Hillary: villages don't exist in America. And if it does take a village to raise a child . . . well, drop your kid off at a mall and he'll quickly learn that community and commodity are not easily discernible from each other. He'll need cash, or at least a credit line, for both.

As Americans scour strip malls in search of what sociologist Ray Oldenburg calls the "third space" – a public place for social interaction that is neither home nor work – corporations are itching to fill the void. The zoning of tract house after tract house over the past forty years has left us with nowhere to socialize, and only Boston Market, and perhaps Blockbuster, to get us through an evening. We experience what the seminal expert on third spaces, Henry Miller, once called "the end of world ambience." France has its cafes, England its pubs, Turkey its coffeehouses, America its . . . Wal-Marts? "Urban renewal" efforts of the '80s failed to recreate third spaces in our cities, and only confirmed what suburbanites assumed all along – our cities are hopeless, and better just to leave them be.

Nevertheless, Americans still need a Cheers, where everybody knows your name, or at least that you like your latte nonfat. We crave culture, but at a bargain rate; we yearn for interaction, but need our space. Consumption remains a leisure activity, but today we are not so foolish to believe that a trip to the mall constitutes solid interaction. And we are less tolerant of the pseudoambience we embraced a decade ago, like a piano player on Nordstrom's third floor, near the lingerie section.

Today, corporations seek to attract the fickle consumer by turning stores into "shopping destinations," where the craving for a third space can be fulfilled without compromising our need for convenience: high ceilings, overstuffed chairs, roomy bathrooms, expansive wood floors, <u>pine tables with products neatly stacked on them,</u> and, of course, the flagship color of the '90s – teal.

Nobody has transformed a store into a shopping destination with more vigor than Barnes & Noble. Those in search of community find it in the straight rows of books, the familiarity in titles, the librarianlike uniforms of the employees, and the reassuring sameness in the adjacent Starbucks cafe. The unrelenting banality of Barnes & Noble – whether in Evanston, or Seattle, or Cupertino, or New York City – is no accident. Sameness has become so expected in American culture that one of Oldenburg's criteria for an ideal third space, that it "fall short of the middle-class preference for cleanliness and modernity," sounds as outdated as his own favorite third space – a corner donut shop. No fat-free muffins there.

"Hand-Crafting Consumer Desire," *by G. Beato*
http://www.microweb.com/traffic/pot_01.html
Suck contributor G. Beato's own contribution to cultural deconstruction: the e-zine Traffic. In this piece, Beato examines the Fall 1995 Pottery Barn catalog, finding in its copy a lexical parallel to the manufactured heritage of its products: *"Indeed, with the practiced efficiency of master furniture-makers, the catalog's wordsmiths expertly construct the following themes in the first six pages: handmade craftsmanship, regionalism and tradition, and to a lesser extent, uniqueness and durability. And then for the next fifty-two pages, these tenacious copy artisans hone, sand, and lacquer their themes into a masterwork of 20th-century advertising. Long before one reaches the final page, it becomes clear that the catalog is not, after all, an antidote to retail homogeneity, but in fact, an outstanding example of one of the discipline's blacker arts: the commodification of authenticity."*

http://www.franchise1.com/comp/dunkin1.html
Information about how to become part of the Dunkin' Donuts franchise family (includes attending Dunkin' Donuts University).

Barnes & Noble has taken the concept of the shopping destination one step further by transforming a franchise into a community – based on the assumption that a community can be built around books. Studies show that a majority of Barnes & Noble shoppers would not normally set foot in a "regular" bookstore, i.e., one filled with dust and clutter and lacking the triumphant displays of William Bennett's latest. Frequenters of Barnes & Noble are made to feel connected to a larger, literary community that spans across America – even if that community is gobbling up *Men Are from Mars, Women Are from Venus.*

The number of books sold through chains like Barnes & Noble doubled from 1991 to 1994, according to the American Booksellers Association, and the rapidity with which Barnes & Noble has spread across the American landscape puts it in a league with other "category killer" stores such as Wal-Mart, Home Depot, and Toys 'R' Us. With 3 million books in print worldwide – 1.5 million in English – and fresh product being manufactured daily, there's no lack of culture to be sold.

Or so Barnes & Noble hopes. Though the company has managed to blend consumerism and culture into a seamless product, arguably its biggest draw is still the 30 percent discount on best sellers. The company's recent print ad campaign, of a figure sitting near an inviting bookshelf filled with rows and rows of titles, with the caption "you don't even need to point and click," is a direct counterpoint to the recent advances of the only company that can feasibly cut into its market share – *Amazon.com.*

With over 1 million titles in its database, *Amazon.com* sells books as commodity, not as warm and fuzzy culture. And with discounts on the top three hundred thousand sellers, same-day delivery, and perks such as book-browsing (real) personal agents and email notification of title availablity, *Amazon.com* is turning web surfers into shoppers (and sellers), not through sofas and lattes and literary events, but through boil-

---

Amazon Associates Program Application

http://www.amazon.com/exec/obidos/ subst/partners/associates/associates .html/6410-4264051-417272

The problem facing web-based megastores like Amazon isn't that the net won't support their crass, Sam Walton approach to marketing; cybercitizens lost the battle against creeping commercialism long ago. Rather, the issue is one familiar to many conquering armies: beating the competition doesn't do you any good if you don't give them a way to join you. Hence, one of Amazon's most ingenious innovations, and its smartest move in co-opting any residual anticonsumerist tendencies that may yet linger on the net: the Amazon Associates program, which allows proprietors of *any* website, from *The Village Voice*'s Literary Supplement to Dave Winer's Creating Killer Websites site, to make a commission off book sales directed toward Amazon from a list of books "recommended" on its own site. As the suits like to say, it's a win-win for everyone, but the experience is more pleasurable for some than for others. For David Siegel, the author of Amazon's number one selling book of 1996, the program offers the opportunity for a kind of auto-stimulation rarely seen outside of kennels.

erplate hard sell. It works, too – revenues have jumped 34 percent per month since the company started little over a year ago.

But as long as the nostalgia for Main Street, USA, remains vivid in the American consciousness, and as long as suburban sprawl remains rooted in isolation, the longing for community will still move product at Barnes & Noble. As the saying goes, nothing happens until somebody sells something.

The Fire This Time

by Ann O'Tate

DID  you **make it** to Burning Man last year? Did you hear it might be the last?

Blowing up on Santa Ana winds from the L.A. Cacophony Society, floating down from Portland like fog, the information fronts converge in San Francisco, resulting in Burning Man rumor precipitate: latest reports have the yearly festival relocating south of the border.

Never fear: Burning Man has survived relocation before. Besides, moving to Mexico is the surest sign that Burning Man is indeed the New American Holiday. (Who knew that the giant sucking sound was really just a greedy inhalation of pot smoke and playa dust?) That, and the fact that you can't launch a search for "sell-out" (+ naked people + co-optation) without hitting at least a couple of sites devoted to this year's crypto-corporate festivities.

Of course, the peculiar affinity of Burning Man's neopagan ritual and the oldest profession's latest incarnation as HTML whore has not gone unnoticed. On the web, picture archives from the Temporary Autonomous Zone threaten to outnumber postcards from the Magic Kingdom, and the haunting homogeneity of both the Burning Man images and the narratives that accompany them speak of product identity and quality control strong enough to make Uncle Walt thaw in his grave. We suspect that it was this trick of self-branding (of a sort more Martha Stewart than modern primitive) that attracted the attention of way-new economists and MTV alike. The only thing that kept Burning Man out of *Business Week* was that no one would admit to making – or seeking – a profit.

Goddamn hippies.

They'll come around. People have been trying to pass off self-marginalization as self-sacrifice for as long as media martyrs have been in vogue (well, at least in *Vanity Fair*), but it's hard for an artist to survive completely outside the mainstream unless he's actually dead. Unable to maintain cred without resisting interviews, unable to eke out a living without granting them, compromised creative geniuses are doomed to a press purgatory, the walking wounded of the alterna-wars.

America's own Miss World said it best when she rode a threat – "You will ache like I ache" – to profitable promise, and a career résumé that can now safely drop dead references. No stranger to suggestions of suttee, we wonder what the widow Cobain would make of recent self-immolations in India, the newly crowned global beauty queen, and her curious, parallel curse to "make the world as happy as I am."

From "Strange Love," by Lynn Hirschberg, Vanity Fair *(September 1992)*
http://hamp.hampshire.edu/~temS95/hole/clc-vf.html
In her strongest song, 'Doll Parts,' she turns introspective: 'I want to be the girl with the most cake/ He only loves those things because he loves to see them break/ I think it's all true – I am beyond fake/ Someday you will ache like I ache. . . . .'

"Get Courtney Love!" by Crystal Kile
http://ernie.bgsu.edu/~ckile/love.html
"She needs shooting, and I'll shoot her."

Some argued that the police crackdown that accompanied the Miss World finals would only fan the flames of protest. Since the coronation went off without a hitch, we have to ask: Whose sari now?

Apparently, the hotel housekeeper is. Irene Skliva, the eighteen-year-old Greek model who won the controversial Miss World crown, greeted reporters in clothes she copped from a chambermaid. It's a twist on the usual Cinderella story, but the traded trousseau probably isn't the kind of cultural exchange that pageant organizers were hoping to highlight.

The businesses that brought these ceremonial pyrotechnics to the subcontinent couldn't have predicted the heated debate that would fol-

"Sell your soul online! Ramp up to the Information SuperHighway to Hell!!!"
http://www.istorm.com/burningman/helco.html
If something as viciously sprawling and anti-centralist as Burning Man could be said to have had a theme, in 1996 the leitmotif of the festival was the fiendishly invasive HELCO. The metaphor of corporatization was, of course, a devilishly clever in-joke for those who believed that the Burning Man festival was either in the process of arriving at or had already arrived into the most heatedly debated circle of hell: the mainstream. Burning Man founder Larry Harvey pointed out in an interview that there is no "magic number" at which the community falls apart, rather, that Burning Man needs to be more selective as community in order to survive as one, Harvey hints at what really bugs people about Burning Man becoming more popular: it isn't that the festival is entering the mainstream, it's that the mainstream is entering Burning Man.

India Web On-Line Magazine

http://pulse.webindia.com/to051004.html

"Farmer's body threatens to torch the beauty pageant venue Karnataka Rajya Raitha Sangh chief M D Nanjundaswamy, who had led a violent campaign against opening of outlets of Kentucky Fried Chicken and Pizza Hut, has now threatened to torch the Chinnaswamy Stadium in Bangalore, which is the venue of the international Miss World beauty pageant.

"Addressing a rally of his activists outside the stadium on Friday, the leader said they would not allow the conduct of the contest in Bangalore under any circumstances and would torch the stadium if Amitabh Bachchan Corporation Limited failed to call off the event.

"He said the show would pave the way for cultural imperialism. The rally was organized by the newly-formed Federation of Opponents to the Miss World Contest."

low. Still, in a country that's seen disasters on a scale most Americans can only conjure in the context of fantasy (and even then, not terribly effectively), resisting cultural destruction might seem like a comparatively easy project; fighting the invasion of Pizza Hut and KFC, which sparked earlier exhortations to go extracrispy, takes on only money and not the megacosm.

What hotheads don't understand is that corporations are the new forces of nature, migrating to wherever the atmosphere is the most receptive, then changing the climate themselves. It's a feedback loop of emissions and permissions, and India's hosting Miss World was an attempt to pitch a tent amidst those gale force winds of change.

Reuters reports that the competition did make some concessions to community standards, but the pageant officials' real interests were thinly veiled indeed: "In deference to Indian mores, the contestants wore long transparent skirts." Onlookers and organizers appear to have missed the point, if not the peep show, for what India really has to fear from Miss World is not the "commercialization of beauty" (a skin trade for which India is already well known) but the beatification of commerce, and the crafty way commodification disguises itself as entertainment or vice. Nothing actually changes about the event, you see – everyone's still naked underneath their clothes.

Defining themselves in contrast to the neon nightlife across the desert, participants at the domestic Burning Man like to think they're gambling with only their lives. However, the amount of energy, time, and money that goes up in smoke in the middle of Black Rock City is a ritual of excess that only late, really late, no-more-snooze-alarm-this-time capitalism could harbor. Affluence has given us the freedom to revert back to nakedness, but all it really celebrates is that we've got money to burn.

The Institute for Global Communications: Environmental Law
http://www.igc.apc.org/elaw/asia/india/ descent.html
This site contains the metaphorically appropriate account of one man's "descent into toxic hell in India." The citizens of the Burning Man camps call their joyfully anarchic mini-states the "Temporary Autonomous Zone," and while the ebullient disregard for governmental authority is cute on a personal level, on a corporate level it is deadly. This article reveals what happens when everyone acts as if they were the only people on the planet: "We entered the industrial factory zone, drove past pharmaceutical companies, chemical plants, fertilizer plants, steel plants, and came to a large, black pool – a small lake, really – that was an unlined pit for toxic waste the color of a moonless midnight."

THE SUCKSTERS

Anonymity has always been a thin veil, and in these days of smart cookies and smarter

marketers, the chances that you can keep your identity to yourself are slimmer than ever. Which is why the Suckster's pseudonyms were never really intended to throw anyone off our scent, but rather to throw them for a loop, distract them from who we are and make them focus on what we're saying. The metatasizing of meta-media has created a boom market in punditry, and Suck was created, in part, to burst that bubble. And while no one believes in the inadequacy of hypocrisy as a critical weapon more feverently than we, it became obvious early on that making a name for ourselves as antipundits meant taking away the names of our selves. That Suckonyms were a way to squeeze one more cheap jape into an already laff-crowded screen was another consideration; and no doubt this was the deciding factor in running pieces by the likes of "Howard Beagle" and "Screed Racer." Still, identity has its merits, especially when it comes to cashing checks.

In order of appearance:

Terry Colon, SWM, cartoonist/designer seeks appreciative, receptive audience with good sense of humor for illustrations in this book. Currently on leave from primary job as Vice President for Life of the Government in Exile of the Republic of Freedonia.

Trademarks of The Soundbitten Corporation, "St. Huck" ("Enema Vérité," "Must-CNET TV?" "Speed Reading Between the Lines," "What's My Line?") and "G. Beato" are interchangeable aliases, designed to encourage notions of authority and individual craftsmanship. Any resemblances to actual persons, living or dead, is coincidental. Soundbitten provides a variety of editorial and broadcasting services, including celebrity ghost-writing, infomercial scriptwriting, greeting card composition, and talk-show media dialysis. Please address all inquiries to *sales@soundbitten .com*.

Screed Racer ("New York Minute"), who also answers to "John Aboud," is a filthy recluse who only leaves his East Village squat to fulfill his obligations as Grand Admiral of the Central Park Model Yacht Club.

Carl Steadman writes unders a host of identities, including Howard Beagle ("Big Money, Little Clue"). He is the cofounder of Suck, and the creator of Placing.

Joey Anuff wishes he'd never heard of the Duke of URL.

Writing under the pseudonym of Ann O'Tate, Ana Marie Cox ("All the World's a Stage," "Fire This Time," "Wiping the Slate Clean") knows no shame, though she may have passed through it on her way to utter humiliation.

Dilettante/Mike Mull ("Ex Libris") writes software in San Diego.

Hans Eisenbeis is the positive re-enforcement behind E. L. Skinner ("Enlightened Self-Disinterest," "Eurotrashed," "Milking It," "To Err Is Human, To Crash Divine"). He prefers the serial comma, and therefore wagers that the *Chicago Manual of Style* would beat the *AP Stylebook* any day of the week with one hand tied behind its back. He edits and produces Request Line *(http://www.requestline.com)* and Twin Citizen *(http://www.twincitizen.com)*, and he's written for Salon, Feed, Outside Online, Minnesota Public Radio, City Pages, and a variety-pack of negligable 'zines. A graduate of Harvard Divinity School, he aims to prove the invaluable irrelevance of a master's degree in theology.

Dr. McLoo ("The Third Time as 'Tragedy'") is known in other circles as Gary Wolf. He works as Executive Producer at Wired Digital.

In addition to his frequent contributions to Suck as LeTeXan, Tom Dowe has written for *The Texas Observer, Wired,* and *Amp (http://www.wrld pwr.com/amp/)*. He lives in Austin, Texas, and is currently at work on a book on new media and historical memory.

Justine is Paulina Borsook ("Nite Crawler," "Sex and the Single URL") *(loris@well.com/www.transaction.net/people/paulina.html)*, basically a very nice girl who doesn't understand why everyone gets so upset with what she writes. For example, she *used* to be the token feminist/humanist/skeptic/Luddite on the masthead of *Wired* magazine. Her fiction, non-fiction, essays, and poetry have appeared in publications as disparate as *Mother Jones, Newsweek, MIT Press,* the 1997 Sundance Film Festival catalog, and *Byte.* She has an MFA from Columbia. Her book-length critique on technolibertarianism is due to be published by Broadway Books in 1998.

As **Polly Esther** ("Mission: Implausible," "Thinking Outside the Mail-box"), Heather Havrilesky has been writing "Filler," a weekly column in Suck, for as long as she can remember, which is not very long. She also writes sappy love songs on her guitar and melts cheese on a daily basis. She's currently working on a field guide to chafing personality types and a rock opera about the horrors of junior high school.

POP, though still involved in the computer industry, is never ever going to work for a start-up again. His former company, as of mid-1997, has yet to go public, leaving his paltry options worth exactly nothing.

Lotte Absence ("Sub-Middle Management Worksick Blues"), daughter of a Japanese chewing gum magnate, married the son of an American diplomatic attaché based in Tokyo during the "boom" years of the 1980s, before eventually moving to America. After stints working in SF's Multimedia Gulch and NYC's Silicon Alley, she has retreated to a small, Northeastern U.S. city that will probably be "discovered" by *Money* magazine as "livable" and by *Rolling Stone* as "The Next Scene Town" by the turn of the millennium.

Steve Bodow records under the name **Johnny Cache** ("To Market, To Market"), and lives in the glamorous Manhattan district of New York City. He also writes for *Details, Feed, Spin,* and sundry other hipster journals. He's Head Writer and Codirector of Elevator Repair Service Theater Co., and proudly holds down a day job as a website editor/producer.

Tom Ace, the brawn behind the brains of **Seymour Cranium** ("A Cross-Eyed Between"), is a writer, editor, and envelope licker at *Diseased Pariah News,* a magazine with a decidedly twisted sense of humor by, for, and about people with HIV disease. He sucks – nay, he swallows. By day, Mr. Ace prostitutes himself as a mild-mannered engineer, writing electronic design automation software for startup companies you've never heard of.

Ersatz ("Wigged Out") is a pale shadow of Sam Pratt, who is CEO, CFO and CIO of E-Z Arts, the multinational media conglomerate which publishes *The Ersatz (The Magazine of Cheap Imitation)*. He knows his 9-digit ZIP code, and yours.

Michael Sippey overshadows **Cleary S. Day** ("An Astral Theory of Rock") as the editor of Stating the Obvious, yet another website offering weekly commentary on Internet technology. In other words, he's nothing more than a new-media-hack wannabe, and would love nothing more than to be quoted as a "pundit." An English major who sold out for dreams of stock options and home ownership, Michael is currently on a quest to invent his own personal business model.

Miss de Winter keeps house as Rebecca Vesely ("Anywhere, USA"). She holds a steady job as the *Wired News* Washington, D.C. bureau chief. She would rather write recipes, though, and has always wanted a pony for Christmas.

AFTERGLOW

All of the essays contained in this book are available online at the *Suck.com* website at the specific URLs listed below. There's a new Suck essay every day and all of them (including those listed here) come in easy-to-print-out, ultra-transportable, cost-free form. Sucker.

"A Cross-Eyed Between," *Seymour Cranium*
>   (http://www.suck.com/daily/96/07/09/)

"All the World's a Stage," *Ann O'Tate*
>   (http://www.suck.com/daily/96/11/12/)

"An Astral Theory of Rock," *Cleary S. Day*
>   (http://www.suck.com/zerobaud/96/08/01/)

"Anywhere, USA," *Miss de Winter*
>   (http://www.suck.com/daily/96/11/15/)

"Big Money, Little Clue," *Howard Beagle*
>   (http://www.suck.com/daily/96/07/22/)

"Character Assassination," *Duke of URL*
>   (http://www.suck.com/daily/96/11/05/)

"Dining with Cannibals," *POP*
>   (http://www.suck.com/daily/96/06/24/)

"Enema Vérité," *St. Huck*
>   (http://www.suck.com/daily/97/02/28/)

"Enlightened Self-Disinterest," *E. L. Skinner*
>   (http://www.suck.com/daily/96/12/16/)

"Eurotrashed," *E. L. Skinner*
>   (http://www.suck.com/daily/96/10/22/)

"Ex Libris," *Dilettante*

(http://www.suck.com/daily/97/03/03/)

"Master of Ceremony," *LeTeXan*

(http://www.suck.com/daily/96/10/18/)

"Milking It," *E. L. Skinner*

(http://www.suck.com/daily/96/11/19/)

"Mission: Implausible," *Polly Esther*

(http://www.suck.com/daily/96/05/15/)

"Murky Brown," *Duke of URL*

(http://www.suck.com/daily/96/03/15/)

"Must-CNET TV?" *St. Huck*

(http://www.suck.com/daily/96/10/09/)

"New York Minute," *Screed Racer*

(http://www.suck.com/daily/96/10/30/)

"NikeTown Crier," *St. Huck*

(http://www.suck.com/daily/97/03/14/)

"Nite Crawler," *Justine*

(http://www.suck.com/daily/96/08/07/)

"OK Marketing," *Duke of URL*

(http://www.suck.com/daily/96/02/14/)

"Search and Destroy," *Duke of URL*

(http://www.suck.com/daily/96/07/16/)

"Sex and the Single URL," *Justine*

(http://www.suck.com/daily/96/06/26/)

"Speed Reading Between the Lines," *St. Huck*

(http://www.suck.com/daily/97/01/06/)

"Sub-Middle Management Worksick Blues,"*Lotte Absence*

(http://www.suck.com/daily/96/08/07/)

"The Fire This Time," *Ann O'Tate*

(http://www.suck.com/daily/96/11/27/)

"The Third Time as 'Tragedy,'" *Dr. McLoo*

(http://www.suck.com/daily/96/11/08/)

"The Writing's on the Stall," *Duke of URL*

(http://www.suck.com/daily/97/01/17/)

"Thinking Outside the Mailbox," *Polly Esther*

(http://www.suck.com/daily/97/01/10/)

"To Err Is Human, To Crash Divine," *E. L. Skinner*

(http://www.suck.com/daily/96/08/12/)

"To Market, To Market," *Johnny Cache*

(http://www.suck.com/daily/97/03/07/)

"Wigged Out," *Ersatz*

(http://www.suck.com/zerobaud/96/08/22/)

"Wiping the Slate Clean," *Ann O'Tate*

(http://www.suck.com/daily/96/06/28/)

There are lots of pages on the web, even more
that used to be there. Other URLs listed in this
book may or may not work, but you can only
blame us – working or not – for these.

PRODUCT PLACEMENT